Bread for the World

by
Arthur Simon
Executive Director of *Bread for the World*

PAULIST PRESS
New York/Ramsey
and
WM. B. EERDMANS PUBLISHING CO.
Grand Rapids

To Peter and Nathan

Graphs numbered 2, 3, 4 and 7 on pages 28, 33, 50 and 134 were prepared by Brenda Roth.

All royalties from the sale of this book will go to the organization Bread for the World.

Library of Congress
Catalog Card Number: 75-16672

Paulist ISBN: 0-8091-2670-2

Eerdmans ISBN: 0-8028-0026-2

Published by *Paulist Press*
545 Island Road, Ramsey, N.J. 07446

and

Wm. B. Eerdmans Publishing Co.
255 Jefferson S.E., Grand Rapids, Mich. 49503

Printed and bound in the
United States of America

Contents

Preface

This book serves as a general introduction to world hunger, but it emphasizes primarily the neglected role of public policy. Millions want to do something about hunger. Few bother with public policy. Yet government policies may multiply or nullify a hundredfold private efforts to assist hungry people. Ordinary persons can help to shape those policies. That is the thesis of this book. Because Christians have a special invitation to care about hungry people, the book is addressed primarily to them, but it is intended also for others.

The United States has never made the elimination of world hunger a priority. It's not that we have done nothing, but rather that what we have done has been here a little, there a little. We have tinkered with solutions instead of making the elimination of hunger a major foreign policy objective.

Presidential leadership in this regard has been dismally deficient for decades, and the record of Congress less than inspiring. No President of either party has put forward a comprehensive set of policies that offer some hope of moving us toward a hunger-free world. The real value of U.S. development aid continues to decline—to cite just one example—and the number of hungry people worldwide is probably increasing.

In short we have drifted and retreated on this crucial issue when we should have been leading the way. Lack of understanding about hunger and its causes, and about how this country is responding, lies behind our retreat. A better understanding would go a long way toward helping the nation reach out to others in a manner worthy of its founding ideals. One purpose of this book, therefore, is to provide people with a clearer picture.

But understanding must lead to action. So the second purpose of this book is to persuade readers that they can bring about important changes by using their leverage as citizens. If enough alert voters in each congressional district began to insist on better policies, our leaders would soon respond. Evidence supports this claim.

This book first appeared in 1975, shortly after Bread for the World was launched as a national Christian citizens' movement. The publication of this revised edition coincides with the 10th anniversary of that movement from which the book's title is taken. Neither edition was written as an academic exercise, but as a call to commitment and action. In this book I appeal to people who want their lives to make a difference, who are willing to prevent unnecessary suffering and death.

Although I wrote at the request of Bread for the World's board of directors (listed in Appendix IV), this book does not represent an official statement of policy. For that, the reader can check Appendix I, bearing in mind that Bread for the World's policy statement is subject to review and change. I have tried to reflect the positions outlined in that statement, but because no two persons will do that in exactly the same way, each reader can make his or her own comparison.

This book represents in part a revision of *The Politics of World Hunger* (Harper's Magazine Press, 1973) which I wrote with my brother Paul, who immersed himself in the issue of world hunger first as a state legislator and more recently as a member of Congress from Illinois. Readers of both books will see similarities. Some of the themes in this one are discussed more fully in the earlier work, so it may have value as a further reference.

I am indebted to those who read all or parts of my manuscripts and offered valuable suggestions: Eugene Carson Blake, William J. Byron, C. Dean Freudenberger, Iqbal Haji, Hulbert H. James, Richard J. Neuhaus, Paul Simon, Carol Simon, and various members past and present of Bread for the World's staff, including Stephen Coats, Barbara Howell, Brennon Jones, Lorette Picciano-Hanson, John Olinger, Paul Nelson, Kim Bobo, Lane Vanderslice, Bob Wilson, Joel Underwood and Bard Shollenberger. Several of them, along with Mary Ruth Herbers, Carla Wharton, Peter Doyle, Kathy O'Pella and Judy Zatsick, tracked down numerous statistics or gathered other information for me; but Anne Crowley carried the burden of that work for my revised edition. Brenda Roth did most of the graphs. Many persons in government, international and private agencies offered extensive assistance. Dolly Youssef, my administrative assistant, deserves special tribute. She not only typed and retyped the manuscript, but her exceptional skill in organizing my work and protecting my time was indispensable and I cannot thank her enough. I am deeply grateful to all of the above persons. None deserves blame for the shortcomings of this book. All deserve thanks.

Arthur Simon
February 1984

Part I

The Struggle for Bread

1
Hunger

In its rawest form hunger is a child with shrivelled limbs and a swollen belly or a person gone blind for lack of vitamin A. But for the most part hunger escapes our notice because it hides behind remarkably ordinary faces: children or adults with no jarring physical deformities. They simply don't have enough food and are therefore sapped of health and energy, and often of hope. Hunger is hidden in the grief of parents, in lost opportunities and in wasted lives.

A single victim of hunger is one too many. But according to the UN Food and Agriculture Organization at least 450 million people in developing countries, excluding China, are malnourished. They consume substantially less food than is needed to sustain life and a normal amount of light activity.

Another estimate comes from the World Bank. The Bank reports that in 1980, again excluding China, approximately 750 million persons lived in "absolute poverty." They constitute one-third of the total population of developing countries. The Bank defines the absolute poverty line as "the income level below which adequate standards of nutrition, shelter and personal amenities cannot be maintained." By doing without necessities such as medical care, clothing, or shelter, some of the absolute poor may obtain an adequate diet; but it is fair to assume that the vast majority are undernourished.

Almost half of these victims are children. As a result, the United Nations Children's Fund (UNICEF) reports that every day 40,000 small children die from malnutrition and infection.

Most hungry people are not starving to death. Starvation is only the extreme form of hunger. Without enough calories the body slows down and becomes weaker—that's hunger. But at some point the body starts to devour its own vital proteins for energy. When this happens, starvation has begun, a process described by *Time* this way:

> The victim of starvation burns up his own body fats, muscles and tissues for fuel. His body quite literally consumes itself and deteriorates rapidly. The kidneys, liver and endocrine system often cease to function properly. A shortage of carbohydrates, which play a vital role in brain chemistry, affects the mind. Lassitude and confusion set in, so that starvation victims often seem unaware of their plight. The body's defenses drop; disease kills most famine victims before they have time to starve to death. An individual begins to starve when he has lost about a third of his normal body weight. Once this loss exceeds 40 per cent, death is almost inevitable.[1]

Unfortunately the U.S. public tends to think of hunger primarily in terms of famines that are dramatic enough to attract media coverage. When these occur, we see on our TV screens the faces of hunger in refugee camps, shanty towns or villages. But famine is merely the tip of the iceberg. Beneath that tip is the far more pervasive and stubborn problem of chronic malnutrition. We can respond to famines by sending emergency food aid, but chronic malnutrition has no simple remedy. For the most part it is invisible. Relatively few victims attract the attention of tourists or television cameras. They suffer in quiet obscurity. Their bodies and often their minds function at half pace. They get sick too often and die too soon. And death seldom arrives as an undisguised case of starvation. Usually it takes the more merciful form of measles or diarrhea or some other disease.

In *Living Poor* Moritz Thomsen, a 48-year-old farmer from the state of Washington, tells of his experience as a Peace Corps volunteer in a remote village of Ecuador. During a drought people in a nearby village "were selling their children before they died of hunger; autopsies on the ones who had died revealed stomachs full of roots and dirt." In his own village, the birth of a stillborn child was occasion for jubilant celebration, since it meant that someone had become an *angelito* without all the suffering.

Thomsen, who paid a village family to let him eat his evening meal with them, describes the pathetic sight of their baby girl, malnourished and sickly, sleeping on the floor during mealtimes, or eating bits of banana or rice off the floor. He received favored treatment as a paying guest, but even that skimpy fare became more meager:

> Instead of fish and rice, we were tucking away *aba* soup, and rice with *abas; abas* being a large, fat, tasteless bean about 200 percent blander than a lima bean. The evening meal became more and more spiritual. A dozen or so times I staggered over to Alexandro's house, ravenous with hunger and anticipation, to find that supper was one well-centered and naked fried egg cowering on the plate. What made even this more or less tasteless was my knowledge that it was the only egg in the house and that the rest of the family was supping on cups of hot water and brown sugar and platano, an enormous, banana-like monstrosity, about 99 percent starch, which was as tasteless as paper. Eating the only egg in the house while the youngest child slowly wasted away from malnutrition didn't help things either.[2]

Thomsen was initially outraged by the apparent laziness of the villagers—until circumstances forced him to eat what they ate. Then he discovered why many of the world's farmers are able to work only three or four hours a day. "There are just so many miles to a gallon of bananas," he observed.

Behind the overpowering, impersonal statistics on hunger are people, real people, suffering and dying because they do not enjoy a basic right that the rest of us take for granted: the right to a nutritionally adequate diet. And these individuals comprise much of the human family.

Hunger is nothing new. Hunger drove the sons of Jacob to Egypt, where "the whole world came to buy corn from Joseph, so severe was the famine everywhere." Famines have occurred throughout history, some of them worse than those of the early 1970s. Yet in the 1970s the world began paying far more attention to hunger. Three reasons account for this:

1. *Although famines have been just as severe before, the famines of the 1970s were more widespread.* Hunger is increasingly determined

by degree of poverty rather than by geography. Famine formerly struck isolated areas; but in the 1970s it touched Asia, Africa and to a lesser extent Latin America.

This occurred partly because bad weather, marked by the shifting southward of the monsoons, affected a thousand-mile-wide strip around the globe, including South Asia and the African Sahel.

Neglect of agriculture and of rural familes—who comprise three-fourths of the population in most poor countries—played a part, as those countries tried to industrialize.

Hunger became more widespread also because of larger increases in the population each year. About 25 million *additional* tons of grain are needed annually just to keep up with population increases.

Another factor, an "affluence explosion," began to rival the population explosion as a pressure on the food supply. The world reached its first trillion dollars in annual income by 1950. By 1975 the world had roughly *tripled* its real income. Most of the increase went to the wealthy northern regions, including the United States, Canada, Europe, the Soviet Union and Japan. People who could afford more meat began to eat more. To the extent that meat comes from animals fed on grain, it corners a disproportionate amount of food. Rich nations feed more grain to their livestock than the people of India and China combined consume directly, and those two countries represent more than one-third of the human race. The "affluence explosion" increased the demand for food and for raw materials that make food production possible, drove prices up, and made food less accessible to many poor people throughout the world.

2. *Another new feature of famine in the 1970s was the growing awareness that hunger can be prevented.* The spread of new farming technologies, the response to famine by the United States and other countries after both world wars, and the rapid growth of transportation and communications all have made a profound impact. Some of the needed technology is available; food can be distributed; and people hear about this. Hungry people hear about it, too. Where once a fatalistic attitude toward hunger and famine prevailed, people now learn that hunger is not inevitable. That helps to explain why representatives of the poor countries insist on making their voices heard in world forums such as the United Nations when trade, food, population, and other hunger-related issues are discussed.

3. *People have become more aware of world hunger also because food shortages elsewhere hit consumers in the United States with soaring prices—illustrating to each of us the interrelatedness of the world food supply.* This was but one piece of rapidly accumulating evidence in the 1970s that supported the idea of *interdependence.* The environmental movement spread this vision. In other ways so did the oil embargo, inflation, resource scarcities, recession, *detente,* and a range of global developments that directly affected our lives.

The link between increasing hunger and growing interdependence clearly stirred the minds and consciences of many U.S. citizens. It began occurring to us that our failure to approach problems from a global point of view may be the other side of our inability to cope with domestic problems. Chronic unemployment, crime, expanding welfare rolls, racial tension, spreading slums, neglect of our rural areas, a loss of confidence in the political process, and the bizarre presence of millions of hungry people in the United States are some of the impasses we face. These problems are not beyond solutions, however imperfect, and our inability to deal sensibly with them indicates, among other things, a faulty perspective. It is as though we are lost in a forest at sundown, surrounded by trees that make grotesque, frightening shadows. What we need to do is to see our place in the woods. *A commitment to the whole world, one which begins at the point of people's need for food, would enable us to gain that perspective.* Solutions will then begin to emerge on some of our own internal problems.

The idea is hardly a new one to Christians, who claim a global citizenship. God so loved the *world,* we affirm, that he sent his only Son to redeem it, a Son who had compassion on the hungry and told his followers to feed them. The famines of the 1970s prompted many believers to take their own faith more seriously in this regard.

The Formation of a Crisis

If the hunger crisis that unfolded in the 1970s illustrates the world's growing interdependence, it also shows that interdependent *action* cannot be taken for granted. If anything, the United States has moved away from such action in recent years, as far as world hunger is concerned.

The U.S. response to the hunger crisis, set in the context of events that preceded it, indicates this.

After World War II the United States gave massive food relief to stricken nations and helped in the reconstruction of Western Europe. Europe's spectacular recovery paved the way for optimism—often misplaced—about opportunities for poor countries. Success in Europe, along with unprecedented economic growth throughout the industrialized world during the 1950s and 1960s, conditioned people to think of "freedom from hunger" as a natural development.

In the early 1950s huge grain surpluses began to accumulate in the United States. To solve this problem, Congress in 1954 enacted Public Law 480, which provided for shipments of surplus food abroad, most for sale on easy terms, but some as outright grants. These shipments reached a peak of almost 17 million tons in 1964, much of it helping to avert massive starvation in India. This ready reserve aided—and also lulled.

Several developments followed. During the last half of the 1960s the Green Revolution, which introduced high-yielding strains of wheat and rice, rapidly increased food production in India and other countries.

While this was happening, the United States gradually reduced its costly grain surpluses.

Then bad weather persisted, first in sub-Saharan Africa, where devastation was slow to catch public attention, and later across the Indian subcontinent.

In 1971 per capita food production dropped by 1 percent in the poor countries. Few noticed. In 1972 an alarming per capita drop occurred: 3 percent in the poor countries as a whole, and 6 percent in the Far East, excluding China. The Soviet Union also had a bad year, but no one knew how bad until in 1972 the Russians secretly bought—at an enormous bargain—19 million tons of grain in this country, plus 11 million tons elsewhere. U.S. surpluses were suddenly wiped out.

Prices soared. The price of wheat tripled. U.S. consumers felt the pinch, but extremely poor people around the world faced a calamity. Many, pushed into the "acutely hungry" category, began spending their entire incomes for food. Some died.

October 1973 brought the oil embargo and the eventual quadrupling of oil prices. This had several consequences. It aggravated a *fertilizer* shortage that had already developed. Even at tripled prices fertilizer was not always available in poor countries. In addition, many farmers in these countries could not get *fuel* for their irrigation pumps. Early in 1974, when many of us complained about waiting a few hours for gas, Norman E. Borlaug, winner of the Nobel Peace Prize for his work on the Green Revolution, saw farmers in India who had waited in line two days with tin containers—but the fuel never came. The price of *pesticides* also rose. Many farmers reverted to less productive, cheaper methods of farming, and food production fell.

In this country also, poor people were the worst victims of rising food costs. Studies showed that less than half of those qualifying for food assistance in the United States received any. By June 1974, testimony before the Senate Select Committee on Nutrition indicated that despite dramatic gains against domestic hunger during the Nixon Administration, many poor people were still hungry and some became hungrier as food prices rose.

The U.S. response to famine abroad was considered critical because more than half of the world's grain exports come from this country. In this respect our control of grain exports is similar to the control over oil exports that countries of the Middle East exercise.

And we cashed in before they did. The food price hikes followed massive Soviet purchases of U.S. grain in 1972. The oil embargo, with a subsequent jump in oil prices, came in October 1973. The United States was vulnerable to the charge of taking advantage of the food crisis. In 1972 this country earned $7 billion in commercial farm exports. By 1974 that figure had passed the $20 billion mark. More significant, earnings from *poor* countries for farm exports jumped from $1.6 billion in 1972 to $6.6 billion in 1974. The $5 billion increase in earnings, almost all accounted for by the price hike, was double the total amount of U.S. non-military assistance to the poor countries that year.

Our position appeared all the more Scrooge-like because of several other factors. For one thing, as U.S. earnings from food sales to poor countries skyrocketed, our food assistance to them dropped sharply, primarily because the dollars we budgeted for food assistance didn't buy as much food. The U.S. cutback forced church and other voluntary agencies doing relief work abroad to cut back, too, because most of the food they distribute is purchased by our government. So while hunger and famine—and our farm export earnings—increased, U.S. food assistance dwindled. It looked like a "sell to the rich and starve the poor" policy.

A second factor put us in a bad light: As food assistance dropped, a larger share of it went to countries in which we had special political and military interests, not countries that needed it most. Secretary of Agriculture Earl Butz said candidly at the November 1974 World Food Conference, where the crisis first fully surfaced, that food is "a tool in the kit of American diplomacy." During the conference he signed a 200 thousand ton food aid agreement with Egypt, where we had a strategic interest, although Egypt was not among the "most seriously affected" nations. In 1974 the United States sent almost five times as much Food-for-Peace aid (Public Law 480 food) to Cambodia, a country with 7 million people, as it did to Bangladesh, a country with 75 million people—even though the need in Bangladesh was far more desperate. The "humanitarian" versus "political" debate prompted one member of the National Security Council staff to argue in all seriousness that "to give food aid to countries just because people are starving is a pretty weak reason." This argument seemed far afield from traditional U.S. generosity.

When the dimensions of the expected famine became clear in November 1974 at the World Food Conference, immediate efforts were begun to fill an emergency "grain gap" that experts agreed would mean the difference between life or death for millions of persons in Africa and South Asia. Speed was critical, because grain shipments were needed during the first half of 1975, and it takes several months to get grain through the "pipeline" to target areas, once a decision to furnish the food has been made.

Immediately after the conference a number of religious leaders and many other citizens urged President Ford to commit at least 4 million additional tons of grain. In February 1975 the President announced an increase of 1.5 million tons (mostly for sale on low-interest terms) to the famine-designated areas. By then India—which had the most extensive shortages—had been forced to use up much of its currency reserves for commercial food purchases. These purchases staved off impending starvation, but invited future hunger because they jeopardized long-range projects such as the development of fertilizer production.

If the unfolding of the crisis shows how interconnected the world's problems are, the U.S. government's initial reactions to it were not encouraging. Our leadership in Washington may never take the far more difficult steps that will be needed to deal with hunger, unless concerned citizens persuade them to do so.

Getting at the Causes

Relief is not enough.

It is one thing to respond to a famine with emergency assistance. It is quite another to get at the causes of hunger with long-range remedies. Both responses are necessary. As the food crisis developed in 1974, many citizens who contribute privately to world relief began asking: "Is this enough?"

They asked it for two reasons. First, they wanted to know what else they could do. Second, they sensed that the problem is so massive that only monumental efforts, aimed at the causes of hunger, will suffice.

Reinforcement for the second idea came in November 1974 when, for the first time, representatives of 130 national governments assembled to deal with the problem of world hunger. They gathered for the World Food Conference. The participation of virtually all national governments dramatized the fact that whatever else hunger is—and it has many complex parts—hunger is also a deeply political issue. It is political not as a form of partisan politics, but in the sense that unless the resources that governments command are brought to bear on world hunger, it can only get worse.

The World Food Conference proposed a *world food reserve program,* coordinated internationally, but with supplies held nationally. The conference set 10 million tons of grain (plus other food commodities) as the lowest acceptable food aid target each year, with a view toward an eventual 60 million ton reserve. By 1984 limited progress had been made on a network of food reserves.

It also asked for a *Global Information and Early Warning System on Food and Agriculture,* now in place, which could identify food shortages in advance and provide public information so that governments can take preventive measures. Access to information is crucial. To cite a famous example, Soviet secrecy regarding its food deficit in 1972 led to huge purchases that caught everyone off guard and greatly aggravated the food shortage.

The World Food Conference also addressed the need for a long-term plan for action. It called for an *International Fund for Agricultural Development* (IFAD) designed especially to help boost the food producing ability, as well as the living standards, of impoverished farm families. With IFAD as a major instrument, the conference hoped to multiply the level of assistance by donor nations for rural development—a goal toward which there has been painfully slow progress. Although IFAD has done an outstanding job of concentrating on the rural poor and obtaining production gains where they are most needed, its 1982 allocation of $339 million was a pittance compared to routine increases in military spending.

In order to coordinate these and related proposals of the World Food Conference, the United Nations established the *World Food Council,* with headquarters in Rome.

The conference also called for broader social and economic reforms that will have to occur within poor countries if hunger is to be noticeably reduced, including land and tax reforms that would benefit small farm holders and landless peasants. At the same time the conference asked for a new economic relationship between rich and poor countries in order to stem the widening economic gap that separates them. This points toward areas such as trade, investment and the monetary system. Actions at this level are often the most important and difficult of all.

The World Food Conference gave us a central insight for responding to the question, "What can I do besides give?" The conference implicitly told the average U.S. citizen: Influence government policy. That answer should not discourage giving—private relief and development projects are needed more than ever—but move us beyond it. Among the various ways in which we can do something about world hunger (see Chapters 13 and 14) the most urgent one is to contact leaders in government on issues that vitally affect hungry people. No personal response is more important.

A single action by Congress or one decision by the President can undo—or multiply—many times over the effect of all our voluntary contributions combined. To make an offering in church for world relief and quietly leave the big decisions up to political leaders only encourages them to make *wrong* decisions. Our silence is taken as indifference or hostility when policies are hammered out, and hungry people become victims.

In the early 1960s John F. Kennedy laid out two goals for this nation: One was to get a man to the moon before the end of the decade; the other was to help eliminate hunger ''within our lifetime.'' We accomplished the first goal, but we moved farther away from the more important goal. Why? In large part because those of us who shared Kennedy's vision of a world without hunger failed to take those simple, responsible steps as citizens to translate the vision into a national commitment.

If we cared, we didn't let our leaders know about it, and they acted accordingly.

Each of us can help to change that.

2
Food Production

Imagine ten children at a table dividing up food. The three healthiest fill their plates with large portions, including most of the meat, fish, milk and eggs. They eat what they want and discard the leftovers. Five other children get just enough to meet their basic requirements. The remaining two are left wanting. One of them manages to stave off the feeling of hunger by reducing physical and mental output, though she is sickly, nervous and apathetic. The other dies from a virus which he is too weak to ward off.

Production and Distribution

These children represent the human family. If present world food production were evenly divided among all the world's people, with minimal waste, everyone would have enough. Barely enough, perhaps, but enough. However, the world's food supply is not evenly divided. The rich fourth of the world produces and consumes more than half of the world's grain. The other three-fourths of the world produce and consume less than half.

You might conclude from this that the problem is one of distribution, and to a large extent it is. The distribution of food among nations and within nations could be greatly improved through various reforms, all of them complex and most of them long-range—such as providing jobs and incomes that would enable the very poor to buy the food they need. To adequately nourish everyone with present levels of production would take a near-utopian arrangement, and even that would not insure enough food for tomorrow. *Hunger is almost certain to stalk the poor countries until they increase substantially their own food production.*

This fact is set against an alarming increase in grain imports by developing countries. Prior to World War II, Africa, Asia and Latin America were all grain exporters. The shift toward more imports was gradual throughout the 1950's and 1960's, but starting in the early 1970's the annual increases began shattering all records. By 1980 developing countries were importing 73 million more tons of grain than they exported. The value of these net imports was about $18 billion, an amount that cut deeply into their own essential development. And in 1981 developing countries for the first time became net importers of *agricultural products*. For many poor countries an increasing dependence on grain imports is like eating seed grain—it serves well for the emergency at hand, but invites future trouble, including the risk of catastrophic famines during periods when global food production drops and the price of grain soars.

Africa faces an especially acute long-term crisis. Of the 37 developing countries whose per capita food production has declined for the past decade or more, 23 of them constitute a majority of African countries. Between 1970 and 1982 Africa's food production per person fell 11 percent. By late 1983 the situation in Africa was further deteriorating as a severe drought ravaged many of those same countries.

U.S. citizens generally recognize the importance of food production in reducing world hunger. In fact technology has such an attraction that we are inclined to depend on breakthroughs in food production, combined with a slowdown of population growth, to solve the problem. Too often writers encourage this viewpoint by dramatizing new technologies in a way that suggests a solution is just around the corner. Or, failing that, they may paint a doomsday picture. Both approaches make exciting copy. But as a result the U.S. public tends to respond to the hunger crisis like a ping-pong ball, bouncing from one oversimplified conclusion to another. When the famines of the early 1970's occurred, the problem seemed beyond hope to much of the nation. Then came a decade of relatively good crops, and the public was beguiled into believing that hunger wasn't such a big problem after all—though the number of chronically malnourished people was probably higher than a decade earlier.

The importance of food production should be underscored. But a single-minded trust in technology fails to take into account its limitations; and such a trust allows us conveniently to by-pass tough social and political decisions that have to be made. The Green Revolution is a case in point.

World Grain Trade
(in million metric tons)

Plus sign shows net exports, minus sign net imports.

Developing Countries by Region	1934–38 average	1960	1970	1980
Africa	+ 1	+ 2	− 5	− 18
Asia	0	− 13	− 22	− 40
Latin America	+ 9	0	+ 4	− 15
TOTAL	+ 10	− 11	− 23	− 73

Other Areas				
Australia and New Zealand	+ 3	+ 6	+ 12	+ 19
Eastern Europe and USSR	+ 5	0	0	− 43
Japan	− 2	− 4	− 15	− 24
North America	+ 5	+ 39	+ 56	+ 132
Western Europe	− 24	− 25	− 30	− 11

Sources: Food and Agriculture Organization and U.S. Department of Agriculture

The Green Revolution

In 1943, with the help of Rockefeller Foundation funds, a research center was opened in Mexico to develop strains of corn, wheat and beans that could increase that country's food supply. Not only has Mexico multiplied its production of these crops since then, but in the mid-1960s a number of Asian countries introduced a Mexican "dwarf wheat" whose thickness of stem and responsiveness to water and fertilizer made possible the doubling and tripling of yields. These gains, along with the development of high-yield strains of rice in the Philippines, gave birth to the Green Revolution. By 1971, 50 million acres—half of these in India—had been planted in new strains of wheat and rice. Several countries, including India and the Philippines, reached the point of self-sufficiency in these grains. This was a striking accomplishment, though self-sufficiency in these cases meant being able to do without imports; it did not necessarily mean raising nutritional levels. In the United States the Green Revolution was widely hailed as the answer to world hunger.

But the poor monsoon of 1972, followed by global shortages of fuel and nitrogen fertilizer, sharply curtailed food production in Asia and elsewhere. Many began to call the Green Revolution a failure.

In fact, the Green Revolution was never intended as a panacea, nor was it the failure that some thought. It did achieve historic gains. It greatly expanded food production and *bought time* for solving other aspects of the hunger problem. It is an on-going revolution, with improved strains constantly being developed. Further, the methods it uses are being applied to achieve similar advances with other crops.

The Green Revolution does not yet, however, offer the technologies needed for tropical agriculture, or even for temperate zone farming over the long pull. Annual cropping ruins tropical soils, which harden in the sun. High-yield farming in the temperate zones depends heavily on fossil fuel and is especially responsive to fertilizer, not sunlight. We need solar sensitive plant and livestock breeding, both for the tropics now and eventually for temperate zone farming, which cannot rely forever on fossil fuel.

But the Green Revolution's most glaring limitation is not technological at all. Experience has borne out an earlier judgment of Addeke H. Boerma, who, as Director-General of the UN Food and Agriculture Organization (FAO), said that the Green Revolution "does not yet have enough of the general economic and social thrust behind it which we have all along said would be necessary and without which it will fail in its broader objectives for bettering standards of life in the developing countries."[1] The main advantages of the Green Revolution have gone to farmers who can afford to invest in seed, fertilizer, irrigation, pesticides and sometimes machines. Unless poverty-stricken farmers are trained in the needed skills and offered credit on fair terms, they may be driven off the land or back to subsistence farming.

So while the Green Revolution does deal effectively with an important aspect of food production *technology*, it does not pretend to answer the underlying *social* problems of reaching primarily hungry, impoverished rural people. Doing that takes quite a different set of decisions than those made by scientists. Much of the needed technology is within reach. But will it be funded? How will it be used? And who will reap the harvest? The answers to these questions depend to a great extent on government policy decisions.

Land

Between now and the turn of the century, three-fourths of the increases in crop production in developing countries will come from higher yields on presently tilled land, rather than by opening new land to cultivation, according to the FAO. In Asia most of the population lives in countries where there is very little potential new land for cultivation. Africa and Latin America have huge reserves of land that could be tilled. But in Africa much of it is tropical and requires jungle clearance, malaria and tsetse-fly control, population resettlement, and a great deal of research to develop food production for the tropics. All of these involve time and money. South America has great tropical forests with their attendant problems for agriculture. It also has ready acreage left idle or underutilized, but sweeping changes in land ownership and taxation are needed before suitable agricultural development will occur.

In short, though the estimates vary, a great deal of land remains to be cultivated. The process will be slow and costly, however; and Asia, which needs land the most, can expect to benefit least from new cultivation. Deforestation in India, Bangladesh and Pakistan increases farm acreage—and flooding—which may result in a net loss. Worldwide, much acreage is lost each year to advancing deserts, soil erosion, overgrazing, and to other encroachments, including suburban developments and highways in our own country. In achieving maximum land cultivation, as much depends upon conservation and restoration efforts as upon tilling virgin soil.

The world turned from new acreage to *higher yields* as the major way of expanding food production in mid-century. By the early 1970s higher yields accounted for roughly four-fifths of the increases worldwide. Japan began moving toward intensive (higher yield) farming in the late 19th century, and the dwarf wheat of the Green Revolution owes its initial success to a gene first isolated in Japan. The United States did not make the transition to intensive farming until after World War II. In his book, *By Bread Alone,* Lester R. Brown reports that corn yields in this country actually declined during the first third of the present century. The use that began in the late 1930s of hybrid corn seed and commercial nitrogen fertilizer has since tripled U.S. corn yields. This U.S. crop alone now accounts for almost one-seventh of the world's cereals and dramatizes the change to high-yield farming.

Soybeans, a high-protein food used mainly in the United States to feed livestock, should provide large gains per acre in the future. High-yielding varieties of soybeans have yet to be developed, but could multiply the output. Another prospect for higher-yield farming is triticale, a tough, productive cross between wheat and rye.

Most gains from intensive farming can and should occur in the poor countries. And it should be *labor*-intensive rather than capital- and energy-intensive, even though capital and energy inputs will have to increase. Asia has only a half an acre of arable land per person, and that ratio is bound to decrease. The experience of China, Japan, Taiwan and others has shown that labor-intensive farming, using the proper inputs and the planting of two or three crops each year on the same land (a method possible in many warmer regions), can multiply the yield. In terms of food production the intensive farming approach, together with gains in tropical agriculture and the development of crops especially responsive to light, offers poor countries their main hope for feeding their growing populations.

Water

The world looks not only to the sky for rain, but also to the oceans and fresh water systems for help in raising food production. Many experts believe that the scarcity of the fresh water supply may do more to restrain food production than the limited supply of land.

Irrigation will expand greatly, but for much of the land presently under cultivation the big irrigation systems have already been developed and in some cases overdeveloped. Not many more deserts are likely to bloom in the next decade or two, because usable water is limited—witness the fight of our southwestern states over rights to existing supplies. Someday the oceans may yield desalinated water for transport to the deserts, but the difficulties and costs now prohibit projects on a massive scale.

The Green Revolution has stimulated emphasis on small tubewells and pumps that farmers can install quickly, rather than on large-scale projects. But even this small-scale technology requires some capital and diesel fuel.

The trend toward small-scale irrigation will gradually be accompanied by a trend toward water-efficient farming as water becomes more scarce. At present, most irrigated land worldwide is devoted to rice, a water-intensive crop. In the future many farmers will turn to crops that use water more efficiently.

Irrigation sometimes brings harmful side effects. Egypt's Aswan Dam has spread a debilitating affliction called schistosomiasis, a parasitic disease carried by snails that afflicts about 200 million people worldwide. The dam has also caused loss of fertility on land previously flooded each year by the Nile. These problems tarnish but do not disqualify the Aswan Dam as a dramatic example of harnessing water to diminish hunger.

Harmful side effects can often be countered. Lester R. Brown describes one instance in Pakistan in which irrigation had waterlogged a wide area of land and spread salt deposits in the soil. These problems were solved by a system of tubewells that lowered the water table by tapping underground water which, when discharged on the surface, washed the salt downward.

Fish

Since 1970, after two decades of rapid increase, the world fish catch has leveled off, resulting in a per capita decline. This has been partly due to the overfishing of many stocks. The cost of fish and competition in the fish industry have increased, as has the human population.

The 1980 world fish catch of 72.2 million tons averaged about 32 pounds (live weight) per person, down from 42 pounds per person in 1970. The distribution of fish is uneven. The United States alone imports about twice as much fish, primarily in the form of feed for livestock, as do all the poor countries combined.

In the long run the fish catch may increase substantially through such means as the expansion of fish farming or with massive catches of krill, a small shrimp-like crustacean. But the case of krill illustrates the underlying problem for poor countries. As one report noted: When krill fishing is finally developed commercially, it is certain to be in the nets of those nations least in need of krill protein—the overdeveloped countries that can afford the enormous expense of mounting Antarctic fisheries—not those that need protein most.[2]

Although fish supply only about 2 percent of the protein in the human diet worldwide, they are still an important source of protein. Better distributed and better used, fish could do much to alleviate hunger.

Fuel and Fertilizer

The connection between food and energy became all too apparent in 1974 when oil and fertilizer shortages aggravated the hunger crisis. The fact that fuel is increasingly needed for food production in poor countries raises serious questions about its use in our own country and its availability worldwide.

The trade-off between energy and food could be agonizing. One acre's corn production requires the energy equivalent of about 80 gallons of gasoline, for example. Conversely, grain can be used to produce fuel—ethanol for use in "gasahol." Either way, we could one day be faced with a choice of consuming energy on highways and in air-conditioned rooms or permitting the production of food to feed large populations in Asia and Africa. The real trade-off exists between the use of energy for essential food production and its use for nonessential purposes. That important distinction receives emphasis from the fact that on-farm use of energy in the United States accounts for less than 5 percent of total U.S. energy consumption.

However, when we move to the entire food system—including the processing, packaging, transportation, retailing, refrigeration and cooking of food—the question of energy trade-offs becomes important. For every unit of energy expended in on-farm production, three units are expended in the processing and distribution of food.

The food system as a whole has become increasingly energy-intensive in the United States. In 1910 that system consumed less energy, measured in calories, than it produced in the form of food calories. But by 1970 the food system required almost nine times as much energy as it produced in food (see the *upper left* side of Graph #1). Corn, soybeans, potatoes, range-fed beef and grass-fed dairy cows still yield more energy than they require in on-farm production (some examples of which appear on the *right* side of Graph #1), but not necessarily when the entire system is taken into account. Most of our corn is fed to livestock, and by the time it reaches our tables in the form of meat, those food calories have consumed their energy equivalent many times over.

Potatoes provide another example. Besides being nutritious, potatoes have good storage qualities and require little processing. But a random visit to a Washington, D.C. supermarket in the summer of 1983 showed fresh potatoes selling for 21 cents a pound, the cheapest french fries for 46 cents a pound, and potato chips 8 to 10 times as much as fresh potatoes per pound, although the fries and the chips have lost much of the nutritional value they had as fresh potatoes. The extra cost supports high-energy processing and, of course, the advertising that coaxes us into buying chips in the first place.

Truck farming around cities used to bring in fresh produce, but suburban developments took over much of that farmland, and we have paid for it in more energy and less taste—greenpicked, refrigerated and artificially ripened tomatoes, for example. Still, the biggest single inefficiency in the farm-to-table odyssey is that of an automobile transporting a bag or two of groceries home.

In a sufficiently energy-abundant world the question of trade-offs between food and energy would not arise. In a world in which energy used inefficiently here could be used in food-deficit areas for food production, the question becomes important.

Less use of energy *here* does not necessarily mean more use *there*, however. The transfer of energy to the poor countries requires devices such as assistance, trade reforms or monetary reforms that would enable

Graph #1: Calories Input to Produce One Calorie Output

Left of the line is the calorie-in to calorie-out ratio of the entire U.S. food system. Right of the line is that ratio for food production only.

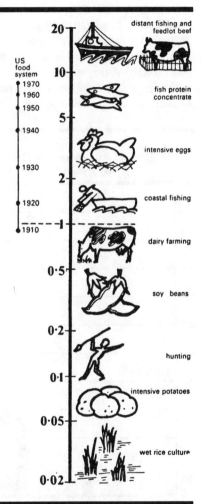

US food system
- 1970
- 1960
- 1950
- 1940
- 1930
- 1920
- 1910

20 — distant fishing and feedlot beef

10 — fish protein concentrate

5 — intensive eggs

2 — coastal fishing

1 — dairy farming

0·5 — soy beans

0·2 — hunting

0·1 — intensive potatoes

0·05 — wet rice culture

0·02

Reprinted from the U.N. *Development Forum,* November 1974.

Source: John S. and Carol E. Steinhart, "Energy Use in the U.S. Food System," *Science,* April 19, 1974.

those countries to purchase the energy, or to develop their own sources of energy.

Commercial fertilizer, the use of which has increased five-fold in the United States since 1950, provides a special link with energy, because nitrogen fertilizer is a petroleum by-product. The importance of fertilizer for poor countries can be seen by the fact that one ton of it, used on depleted soil there, may result in an additional 10 tons of grain, while an extra ton on already fertilized land in our own country will induce a much smaller increase in yield. But, as graph #2 shows, the use of fer-

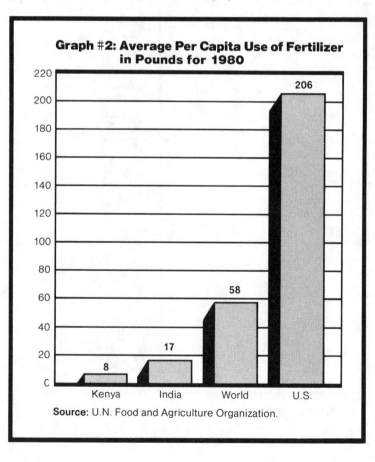

Graph #2: Average Per Capita Use of Fertilizer in Pounds for 1980

	Kenya	India	World	U.S.
Pounds	8	17	58	206

Source: U.N. Food and Agriculture Organization.

tilizer is concentrated in countries with purchasing power, not in those with the greatest need for more fertilizer.

What about the Future?

The biggest and most substantial gains in food production probably lie ahead. The evidence so far, however, tells us to expect most of these to occur along fairly conventional lines, as in the Green Revolution. A similar revolution occurring in tropical agriculture would be an enormous contribution, and it may not be many years away. The use of tropical grasses for beef and dairy cows would be greatly enhanced if tropical diseases could be brought under control. Krill in the Antarctic, triticale on the plains, cereals that can produce nitrogen in the soil, and high-yield soybeans for human consumption grown throughout the world are some other possibilities for food production gains. The development of high-protein cereals and root crops would be especially desirable, because diets for many people in the world have become more protein-deficient—partly because of a trend toward less acreage in beans and peas in several Asian countries.

These gains will take time, however. With 450 million or more people chronically undernourished and 82 million additional mouths to feed each year, time is a major factor.

Nonconventional high-protein foods are certain to become increasingly important, but research and production still present formidable obstacles. Single-cell protein, new forms of food from the sea, the turning of starch into protein, the extraction of edible proteins from ordinary grass and leaves—these and other pioneering efforts deserve more support than they are getting. But the fate of the world's hungry is almost certain to depend for a long time on less exotic methods of production.

Produce they must. The developing countries will have to increase their food production by substantially more than their 3 percent annual average between 1960 and 1980, simply to keep pace with demand and to reverse the trend toward ever more imports. That is a tall order. And it is unlikely to happen unless, among other things, the United States and other nations multiply their assistance for rural development abroad.

More than Technology

René Dumont and Bernard Rosier dedicated *The Hungry Future:*

To the children of backward countries who never
attain their full promise,
or who have died of kwashiorkor,
because the fish meal which might have saved them
has fed the chickens gorged by the rich.

As the last two lines imply, it will take much more than food production to deal with world hunger. Peru's anchovy fishmeal industry, the largest in the world, manufactures high-protein flour not for hungry Peruvians, but for shipment to Europe and the United States where it feeds live-stock. The fact that Peru needs export earnings so badly that it feels compelled to supply protein to well-fed foreigners, while bypassing its own ill-nourished people, tells us that technology is not the whole an-swer to the hunger problem. Social and economic remedies are no less essential.

Africa's food crisis in the early 1980's, for example, stemmed not only from severe droughts, but even more from such factors as soaring oil costs, depressed prices for the agricultural products and minerals that developing countries export, a world economic recession, rapid popu-lation growth and government policies that tend to neglect small scale farmers.

Or consider a poor tenant farmer in India who cultivates several acres in one or more patches. He works with primitive tools and scav-enges manure, not for fertilizer but for fuel. Without irrigation he de-pends entirely on the rains for a harvest. When the harvest comes, half goes to the landlord, some is stored for food, some for seed, some pays off debts, and whatever remains (if any) is sold to a middleman—who may also be landlord and loan shark—at a deflated price. In a case like this both poor technology and social obstacles hinder food production. They perpetuate inequalities and reinforce hunger.

Reflect on the fact that in poor countries as a whole, women ac-count for at least half of the food production. Yet women bear an undue share of the world's hunger and poverty. Their literacy rate is far lower than that of men, their opportunities fewer. They, too, illustrate that hunger is a social as well as a technological problem.

In a different way, U.S. agricultural trade illustrates the role of economic policy in food production and hunger. An oversupply of grain in the United States may generate pressure on our government to promote sales by subsidizing grain exports to developing countries. But doing so slows food production there because cheap food undercuts local farmers. Developing country governments are often eager to set food prices artificially low in order to pacify urban dwellers and prevent social unrest. But doing so undermines their farmers by removing incentive for them to produce more food. For the same reason food aid, if it is not subject to strict conditions, can also depress prices and hinder food production.

Policies on grain reserves also show that hunger is more than a question of production. Without an adequate system of reserves both farmers and consumers are whiplashed by boom-and-bust cycles, as food prices tumble when crops are abundant and soar when crops are poor. Properly functioning grain reserves mean greater food security and less hunger.

Private companies can make an important contribution to food production, but they do not know how to sell food to people who are too poor to buy it. Nutritionist Alan Berg has concluded that "corporate technologists have not yet been able to come up with a high-protein food that can be sold commercially for a profit and still be priced low enough to reach and help the masses of people who most need it."

Hunger does not stand alone. According to Addeke H. Boerma, head of the FAO:

> It would be futile and unrealistic to attempt to discuss hunger and malnutrition in isolation from other evils of our age such as the stifling clamp of poverty, the flood of overpopulation, the paralysis of unemployment, the deformities of trade. We must look at the economic and social problems of the world in their totality if we are to come to grips with them individually.[3]

Overcoming hunger, then, means more than increasing food production, crucial as that is. We also need to sort out hunger's social and economic allies and deal with them in a comprehensive way. To that task this book now turns.

3
Population

"Why don't people in poor countries quit having so many children? The only solution to the hunger problem is birth control!" writes a mother from the Bronx to Bread for the World, a Christian citizens' movement.

Her letter echoes the thoughts of many. It sounds persuasive. But the argument contains one fatal flaw: It ignores the crucial role that hunger plays in spurring population growth. No country, including our own, has ever restrained a population boom without progress in freeing people from the grip of hunger and poverty. Unless that happens, family planning programs make little impact.

Why?

In most poor countries surviving sons take care of their parents in old age. Faced with a high death rate, and starvation never far away, parents know that many children, especially sons, mean security later on. According to India's former Minister of State for Family Planning, hunger induces women in his country to produce from eight to ten children on the assumption that only three will live to become breadwinners. So the vicious cycle of hunger = more people = more hunger continues to worsen.

The idea that the circle can be broken with family planning measures is a fantasy of the rich world. Paul Ehrlich, whose book, *The Population Bomb,* did much to nourish that fantasy, has since ridiculed it as a " 'condoms from helicopters delusion'—a psychological condition that is rampant among well-meaning upper-middle and upper class Americans."[1] He now maintains that as long as poor couples need sons for future security, family planners' propaganda to "stop at two" makes no sense to them. First, Ehrlich says, social changes must occur that make fewer children seem desirable.

A bit of historical background sheds light on this insight.

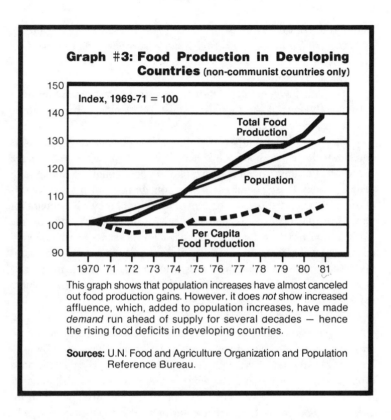

Graph #3: Food Production in Developing Countries (non-communist countries only)

Index, 1969-71 = 100

Total Food Production

Population

Per Capita Food Production

1970 '71 '72 '73 '74 '75 '76 '77 '78 '79 '80 '81

This graph shows that population increases have almost canceled out food production gains. However, it does *not* show increased affluence, which, added to population increases, have made *demand* run ahead of supply for several decades — hence the rising food deficits in developing countries.

Sources: U.N. Food and Agriculture Organization and Population Reference Bureau.

Roots in the West

Almost two centuries ago, in 1798, an Englishman named Thomas Malthus warned that the population would race ahead of the food supply. It would do so, he argued, because we can only *add* to the food supply, while the population *multiplies*. At that time the world's population of less than one billion was growing at a rate of about one-half of 1 percent annually. Now the growth rate is about 1.8 percent for the world and 2.0 percent for developing countries as a whole. These percentages may seem small, but the increase makes a dramatic difference.

By 1930 the world had two billion people. If you were born in 1930, the world's population has already doubled within your lifetime.

And if you live to the turn of the century, *the earth's living population will have tripled history's previous total achievement*—all in one lifetime.

That is an explosion.

It explains why the population graphs show a horizontal line veering suddenly upward—as though a cyclist, riding along a barely noticeable slope, began pedaling straight up a cliff.

The world is presently adding 82 million persons each year to its numbers—the equivalent of the entire U.S. population every three years. Most of this growth is taking place in poor countries among poor people. Today those countries already contain more than three-fourths of the earth's population. By the turn of the century they will account for more than four-fifths of the human race. All the while demand for the world's food supply will climb sharply each year, and—barring unprecedented global efforts—increasing numbers will wind up in the "hungry" category. No wonder the mother from the Bronx and a great many other U.S. citizens are saying: "The only solution to the hunger problem is birth control."

Consider the evidence, however:

Lower death rates, not higher birth rates, are responsible for today's population growth. Poor countries as a whole have actually lowered their birth rates over the past several decades—but death rates have dropped more sharply, and that achievement has touched off the population boom. Advances in medicine and public health, along with increases in food production, account for most gains against early death. For example, while Malthus wrote his *Essay on Population,* a fellow Englishman named Edward Jenner was discovering a vaccination for smallpox. This discovery foreshadowed a long series of steps in disease control that cut back death rates.

The population explosion began in Europe. Not the "inconsiderate poor" of Asia, Africa and Latin America, but white Westerners touched it off. A few simple statistics show this. In 1800 about 22 percent of the human race was Caucasian; but by 1930 (only five or six generations later) that percentage had jumped to about 35. This happened because the new technologies that pushed back the death rate occurred in the West. During that time the white, European peoples had two enormous advantages:

1. *Industrial growth kept ahead of population increases.* Because

gains in public health occurred gradually, population growth rates also increased gradually. The Industrial Revolution had begun earlier, so the population increase was usually needed in the cities by industries, which depended upon a growing supply of unskilled workers. Although the Industrial Revolution imposed cruel hardships on those who moved from farms to sweatshops and urban slums, the suffering would have been greater and the social situation far more explosive had the population raced ahead of industrial jobs. But the jobs usually got there first.

2. *New lands opened up for colonization.* New lands, including North America, offered an important outlet to population stresses that did develop. For example after the potato famine ravaged Ireland in the 1840s, almost a million Irish came to our shores within five years. When periods of unemployment occurred, new lands provided a place to seek work. They also handed European peoples an impressive psychological advantage by keeping hopes alive.

Poor nations face a sharply different situation today. Two centuries of public health gains were made available to them more rapidly, so their populations began to soar almost without warning. Their people now pour into the cities long before industries can possibly supply them with jobs; and for all but a few there simply is no frontier, no new lands to colonize, no safety valve.

Population growth was cushioned in the West (1) because the death rate receded gradually, and (2) because people became economically more self-sufficient and less dependent upon their offspring for security. Today's poor countries have moved quickly into the first stage: Public health measures and modern medicine have reduced the death rate much faster than in the West, causing their populations to multiply more swiftly. *But the second stage has not taken firm hold.* A majority of people in the poor countries do not seem convinced that their security is clearly related to having fewer children. Instead, the opposite too often applies: more children mean more security.

Poor countries can thank us for the population explosion, because rich nations transferred the health technologies that touched it off. But we have not done much to help them develop economies that can absorb new workers and provide positive incentives for small families. We brought them to stage one (a relatively easy task) and largely deserted them in stage two (a far more complicated matter).

To a remarkable extent Malthus has triumphed, because the population is multiplying beyond his wildest fears. Malthus did not foresee how science and technology would cut back the death rate and increase food production.

But in another sense Malthus had things backward. He considered poverty, disease and hunger important though regrettable checks on population growth. So he assailed English welfare legislation (called "poor laws") on the grounds that they only encouraged the poor to have more children. However, history has since contradicted Malthus. Where people are poor, diseased and hungry, the population soars. Disease and infant mortality have been restrained enough in underdeveloped areas to multiply growth rates—but not enough to assure parents that sons will survive to care for them in later years.

Once a country begins to reduce its death rate, it *has* to go on to reduce hunger and poverty as well, or face a runaway population. *Only where the benefits of healthy economic growth are spread among the poor, and where the rate of infant mortality approaches that of the rich nations, do people feel secure enough to have small families.* This happened in our own country, in other industrialized countries, and it is beginning to happen in a few countries that are successfully developing. Adequate nutrition, health care, literacy, and improved incomes for the poor emerge as the most fundamental remedy to the population problem.

This does not minimize the importance of family planning. Nor does it ignore the possibility that disaster or deprivation can, under special conditions (that of Ireland following the famine, for example), provide incentive for smaller families. It does, however, affirm that no country has yet brought a rapidly growing population into balance primarily by promoting private methods of control. Conceivably, of course, pressures of growth combined with improved birth control methods could change that. During 1965–70 the annual population growth rate in developing countries as a whole peaked at 2.4 percent and had dropped to 2.0 percent for the 1980–85 period, a significant decline. Demographers are investigating the reasons for this decline, but it is fair to assume that a drop in the infant mortality rate and longer life expectancy in low-income developing countries (see the next chapter) are major factors. Meanwhile, the evidence tells us that to expect poor countries to solve their population problems primarily by emphasizing family planning is to cherish an illusion.

Some Examples

The experience of poor countries over the past several decades is revealing. Those that have substantially lowered high population growth rates are countries in which the poor have noticeably improved their living conditions. Countries, however, in which the poor remain just as poor and the hungry just as hungry are stuck with stubborn growth rates—regardless of whether birth control measures are pushed or not.

China and India, which together account for 38 percent of the world's population, deserve special mention. Both are economically poor. But China, with more than one billion people, has distributed its resources so that food, housing, health care and education are made available to all. According to reports (which are far from complete) China has largely, though not entirely, eliminated hunger. China's growth rate was 1.4 percent in 1982. That is remarkably low for a developing country, but enough to add 15 million to China's population that year and alarm Chinese officials. China's reduced growth rate and its goal of permanently limiting the total population to 1.2 billion by the year 2000 are based on a spartan system of economic security along with stringent social and economic pressures on parents to stop after one child and face sterilization after two children. Achievement of the goal appears to depend upon authoritarian measures that exact an astonishing cost in human rights.

India, the first developing country officially to promote family planning programs, had an annual growth rate of 1.9 percent for the 1980–85 period, down from a high of 2.3 percent in the late 1960's. By the government's own standard, almost half the population falls below the poverty line, which in 1980 was approximately $11 a month for an urban dweller and $9 a month for a rural dweller. Undernutrition, unemployment and illiteracy are still common, despite overall economic gains. Within India several states—including Kerala, one of the poorest—have cut back the population growth rate significantly, and these are the ones that show exceptional evidence of reducing hunger, making health care available, and increasing the rate of literacy.

In South Korea and Taiwan, birth rates dropped sharply as living standards began to improve, and this happened in advance of active family planning programs. For example, Taiwan's birth rate fell from 46 per thousand in 1952 to 31 per thousand in 1963. That year Taiwan launched an official birth control program, and by 1980 the birth rate had dropped to 23 per thousand. The decline since 1963 may be due more to further economic gains than to the promotion of family planning, though presumably both factors made a difference.

Many countries have higher per capita incomes, but poorer distribution of incomes and social services than South Korea and Taiwan. Consequently they also have higher population growth rates. In 1971 Brazil's per capita income was $395, South Korea's $280. But in Brazil the income ratio of the richest 20 percent to the poorest 20 percent was 25 to 1, while in South Korea the ratio was only 5 to 1. Brazil also had higher rates of illiteracy, infant mortality and unemployment. Both countries had population growth rates of 3 percent in 1958, but by 1971 Brazil's held at 2.9 percent, while South Korea's had dropped to 2 percent. South Korea had the advantage of a birth control program, but, like Taiwan, most of its drop coincided with economic gains by the poor and came *prior* to the program.

What should poor countries do about their rapid population growth? Your answer may depend on where you live. In September 1966, the Committee for Economic Development issued two reports that dealt with the problem. The report prepared by a committee of 44 North Americans urged birth control programs. The other, prepared by nine Latin Americans and one U.S. citizen, favored improved nutrition and reduced infant mortality—with the U.S. member registering the lone dissent. Commenting on these reports environmentalist Barry Commoner notes:

> . . . the Latin Americans wish to pursue, for themselves, the course toward population balance that the advanced nations have followed—increased living standards, reduced mortality, followed by the commonly experienced reduction in birth rate. For their part, the North Americans are urging on the poorer nations a path toward demographic balance that no society in human history, certainly not their own, has ever followed. . . .[2]

An even more striking example of the "here" versus "there" perspectives emerged in 1974 at the UN-sponsored World Population Conference held in Bucharest. The United States strongly urged poor countries to push family planning programs, warning that they would become mired in permanent hunger and poverty, and that the earth's carrying capacity had limits.

Poor countries, on the other hand, argued that social and economic improvements were the key factors, understandably preferring to deal with population growth the way the developed countries have. Representatives of the poor countries pointed out, sometimes scathingly, that excessive consumption practiced by the rich nations contradicted their preachments about the care of the earth. Numerically, population increases are greater in the poor countries, they observed; but in terms of resource-consumption and pollution, growth in rich nations takes a much greater toll. "You want us to cut back on population?" some asked. "Then you cut back on consumption."

The U.S. position at Bucharest contained valid points; but they would have gotten a more receptive hearing if they had been placed within the context of urgent development needs in the hungry world. Not doing so has been, as the mother from the Bronx illustrates, a national blindspot. At Bucharest the United States stood almost alone in failing to see the connection between motivation for smaller families and social-economic development.

The evidence leads us neither to minimize the problem of population growth, nor to downgrade the importance of family planning. But it does warn us against dealing with population growth as an isolated problem, apart from the hunger and poverty that induce such growth. If we are serious about dealing with the population problem, our sensible course, as a nation, would be to take a whole network of actions designed to let people work their way out of hunger and poverty.

Within the framework of such a commitment several points deserve emphasis. First, the elimination of hunger and poverty within our own borders must be part of a global effort to slow population growth. Second, we need to reassess a way of life in which excessive consumption has become a national addiction that engulfs us all and strains the carrying capacity of the earth no less than population increases do. Third, we could invest in more research to develop quickly birth control methods that are dependable, inexpensive, simple, and morally acceptable to all.

But the main point is that efforts to bring the population growth rate

down will be effective only as part of an overall assault on world hunger
and poverty.

"Lifeboat" and "Triage"

How many people can the world adequately sustain? No one really
knows. Much depends on undiscovered reserves, alternate sources of
energy, new technologies, our ability to change patterns of living, and
other factors that prompt a variety of guesses. This uncertainty provides
a field day for alarmists. If you conclude that the earth already has too
many people, your solution is apt to be a bit reckless—as two widely
discussed arguments show.

One, made popular by scientist Garrett Hardin, pictures the rich
countries as lifeboats filled to near capacity. If more people are pulled
in, the lifeboats will sink and everyone will drown. So those in the lifeboats have to push away others who are trying to climb in. By this view,
to feed the hungry and bring them medical care is to overload the lifeboats and, therefore, precisely the wrong thing to do.

The other argument, suggested by William and Paul Paddock in
their book *Famine 1975!,* uses a military idea called "triage." The
world is like a battlefield covered with wounded soldiers, but not enough
medics. What to do? (1) Some will die no matter what help they get.
Abandon them. (2) Others can survive without treatment. Ignore them,
also. (3) Help only those wounded seriously who can be saved by immediate care. Applied to the hunger-population dilemma, a triage means
deciding which countries are beyond assistance and letting their people
starve.

But do these metaphors apply? Why lifeboats instead of luxury lin-
ers to illustrate the rich nations, for example? Triage, the more sophisticated of the two, has rightly been called by *The New York Times* "one
of the most pessimistic and morally threadbare intellectual positions to
be advanced since the demise of the Third Reich." According to the
same *Times* editorial, "the world has yet to make a really serious effort
to crack the food crisis."[3] It points out that starvation prompts a compensating rise in birth rates, while assistance to small farmers and landless laborers results both in more food and in a lower birth rate.

Behind the lifeboat and triage theories lie some frightening, unspoken assumptions about the value of life. Is a hungry, impoverished Asian child less human, with less reason to live and less right to live, than our own children? Playing God in this regard is especially dangerous because we are easily seduced by answers that protect our own advantages, even if they cost lives. Those who believe each person to be an incredibly precious human being, created in the image of God and redeemed by him at great cost, will see in population growth not merely problems, but persons: children of God.

The population growth rate *is* a critical problem, but we can deal with it in a way that affirms and celebrates life. So far, the most effective way to bring the growth rate down has been to bring down hunger and poverty. That requires development efforts that are linked to the aspirations of poor people. And such efforts in turn call for major legislation by Congress to carry out the objectives of its own Right to Food resolutions.*

*See appendix II.

Part II
Bread and Justice

4
"Haves" and "Have Nots"

We will not deal effectively with hunger through private acts of charity alone. It is possible for us to feed a hungry family or two—an action not to be despised—without disturbing the conditions that brought about their hunger. In order to make lasting gains against hunger, the concern from which charity flows must also give rise to justice.

Put another way, we should care enough about hungry people to ask *why* they are hungry. And if we ask that question, the answer is as simple as it is complex: People are hungry because they are poor. We cannot come to terms with hunger unless we deal with poverty. And we cannot understand poverty apart from a rapidly growing gap between the haves and the have nots of the world.

Their Poverty and Ours

Poverty in most countries defies the imagination. Peter Drucker has said:

> What impresses the outside world about the United States today is not how our rich men live—the world has seen riches before, and on a larger and more ostentatious scale. What impresses the outside world is how the poor of this country live. "Up to Poverty" is the proper slogan. . . .[1]

Drucker has a point. Where in our own cities do you see—as you can in India—people carrying buckets of water from or bathing at public water taps, emaciated cattle wandering in the streets, women scooping up piles of dung for use as fuel, children picking out undigested grains from the dung for food, people sleeping in the streets, urinating in the streets, begging in the streets, competing for garbage in the streets, and dying in the streets? British journalist Dennis Bloodworth tells of the time he first brought his oriental wife Ping to London. "Don't show me more museums," she told him. "Show me poor people. I want to see how poor people in West live." So Bloodworth showed her the slums of London, only to find her exasperated. "No," she protested, "You don't understand, I mean poor people, *reary* poor people."[2]

In ordinary times really poor people go hungry. When the price of food goes up, their ranks swell and deaths increase. The list below[3] shows the average percentage of total expenditures that people from various countries paid for food in 1979:

United States	12.7	Zambia	40.4
Great Britain	17.3	Venezuela	40.5
Japan	21.5	Honduras	53.6
Soviet Union	33.7	India	55.5

More is at stake than percentages. Fifteen percent of a $20,000 family income is one thing; but 60 percent of $600 is quite another.

Why Poor Countries Cannot Repeat Our Experience

Not only is the poverty of most nations far worse than poverty within the United States, but today those countries cannot hope to climb to prosperity by duplicating our experience, because the experience of the Western world has been misleading. There is no use telling them: "Do it the way we did it." Scientist George A. Borgstrom points out:

No group of individuals ever seized a greater booty than did the Europeans who took possession of the vast forests and rich prairie soils of the North American continent. Unassuaged, the white man also grabbed the fertile pampas and most other good soils in Central and South America, the South African veld and the rich highland plateaus of the interior Africa. He managed to gain control of an entire continent, Australia, with its valuable satellite, New Zealand. In addition, he secured strongholds all over Asia where he monopolized trade and to a considerable degree controlled agricultural production. . . .[4]

Grade school history lessons about conquerors, colonizers and empire builders taught us how European people gained control of most of the world by the turn of this century. We learned this and took it in stride, forgetting that the same history had quite a different meaning for those who were conquered. For example, Bengal (today's Bangladesh and the West Bengal state of India), the first territory that the British conquered in Asia, was a prosperous province with highly developed centers of manufacturing and trade, and an economy as advanced as any prior to the industrial revolution. The British reduced Bengal to poverty through plunder, heavy land taxes and trade regulations that barred competitive Indian goods from England, but gave British goods free entry into India. India's late Prime Minister Nehru commented bitterly, "Bengal can take pride in the fact that she helped greatly in giving birth to the Industrial Revolution in England." British rule became comparatively enlightened and brought some advances to India such as Western science. But, as India illustrates, the North Atlantic powers seized territories and privileges to enrich themselves, not to benefit the local population.

New lands not only boosted Western economies, but they also provided a safety valve for Europe's growing population. We can imagine the burden for Europe if all its living descendants—virtually the entire population of the United States, Canada, much of Latin America, plus Australia and some European colonies in Asia and Africa—were compressed into Europe. North America in particular was a huge breadbasket waiting to be farmed, a storehouse of natural resources made to order for the Industrial Revolution.

Lester B. Pearson, the late Prime Minister of Canada, reminds us what a difference these advantages made when the North Atlantic nations were struggling to develop:

> One hundred fifty years ago, most economists doubted the capacity of the new Atlantic-European industrial system of that epoch to survive. What transformed mid-century gloom into the long Victorian boom was, above all, the opening up for

settlement by Atlantic peoples of the world's remaining, virtually unoccupied belt of fertile temperate land. This biggest
bonanza ever bestowed upon a single group was purchased for
little more than the cost of running the Indians and the Aborig-
ines and the Bantu off their ancestral lands. It temporarily
ended the Malthusian nightmare of population growth out-
stripping resource availability. Its vast input of almost "free"
resources took the Atlantic countries past the borders of mod-
ernization and into the new territory of "sustained growth."
Nothing comparable is available to developing nations today—unless we use our abundant capital and technology to
provide a comparable form of aid relevant to our times. If we
say they must develop without it, then we are really abandoning them to permanent helplessness and poverty.[5]

Pearson adds, "Their nineteenth century bonanza gave the Atlantic peoples, representing less than 20 percent of the world's population, a grip
on the planet's resources which they have since maintained and even
strengthened."

Today's poor nations have no comparable outlet for their populations, which are increasing far more rapidly than Europe's ever did.
They do not have the input of wealth, science and energy that characterized growth in Europe and North America, an input obtained in part at
the expense of the poor nations. They face the difficult task of pulling
themselves up from poverty at a point in history when forces threaten to
suck them deeper into it.

In these countries most migration occurs not to lands of opportunity, but to cities of last resort. Until recently cities in Europe and North
America grew along with industries that supplied jobs. But poor countries now experience the opposite: peasants pour into cities far in advance of employment opportunities. Too few industries exist, and some
hire only skilled workers because they are already automated. "Hands"
are no longer as marketable as they were earlier in our own history.

Most U.S. citizens clearly build on unparalleled advantages. The
merchants, farmers, factory workers, and housewives of our country enjoy a level of prosperity that is possible only because the past has granted
us unprecedented favors. We have been living off the labor and resources of others more than we realize. Inherited economic and social

advantages, not moral superiority, explain why the average personal income (after taxes) in the United States reached $8,906 in 1981, a figure that amounted to $35,624 a year for a family of four. Because earnings are unevenly distributed, a majority of U.S. families earned much less than that. The fact remains that hungry people of the world do not have the advantages that paved the way for these achievements.

A Widening Gap

In comparing rich and poor nations today we are pressed to use the crude measuring device of either per capita national production (GNP) or per capita income. But this country's GNP includes research and development of highly polluting technologies, as well as the cost of repairing the environmental damage caused by those technologies. Both are counted as part of the nation's output, although one should be subtracted from the other. Similarly, traffic jams raise the GNP by boosting gasoline sales, auto repairs, and medical expenses. GNP figures may also distort in the sense that a haircut in the United States may cost ten times the price of a haircut in India—but a haircut is a haircut. Despite these distortions, GNP figures provide us with a fairly clear idea of where wealth and poverty are concentrated. They tell us that in 1981 the richest fourth of the world had 78 percent of its GNP. The other three-fourths had the remaining 22 percent.

Other disparities between the developed and developing countries are shown in graph #4. The graph, however, does not distinguish between low-income developing countries—which include China and India and account for almost two-thirds of the developing country population—and more prosperous developing countries. For example, the 1981 average per capita GNP for low-income developing countries was $272, compared with $772 for developing countries as a whole. Low-income developing countries account for more than half of the world's population, but less than 10 percent of its GNP.

The contrast between rich and poor nations is illustrated by the simple fact that New York City's 1984 budget was almost half the size of India's national budget, although India with a population of more than 700 million has a hundred times as many people as New York City.

More distressing than the *size* of the gap between rich and poor na-

Graph #4: The Development Gap

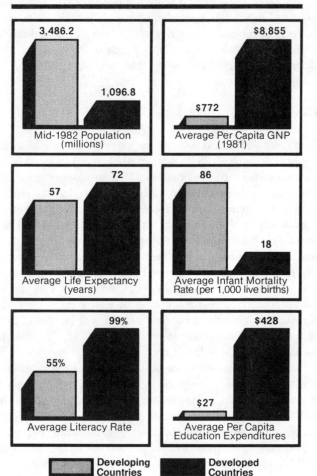

3,486.2	$8,855
1,096.8	$772
Mid-1982 Population (millions)	Average Per Capita GNP (1981)
72	86
57	18
Average Life Expectancy (years)	Average Infant Mortality Rate (per 1,000 live births)
99%	$428
55%	$27
Average Literacy Rate	Average Per Capita Education Expenditures

Developing Countries   Developed Countries

Source: Overseas Development Council, **U.S. Foreign Policy and the Third World Agenda 1983,** John P. Lewis and Valeriana Kallab, ed., Praeger, NY, 1983, pg. 207.

tions is that the gap continues to increase. Two centuries ago the average per capita income of the richest countries was perhaps eight times greater than that of the poorest. But today's average U.S. citizen has an income level almost a hundred times that of his or her counterparts in Bangladesh. The gap has widened in recent decades. Compare the growth in per capita income* between India and the United States:

	India	United States
1953	$ 64	$1,581
1973	100	4,315*
1981	260	8,906*

There is virtually no chance of narrowing the gap in total dollar amounts for many years. Doing so would require almost no real economic growth in the rich countries, a situation that would almost certainly set poor countries back even further. Per capita income in the United States is about 34 times that of India. A 1 percent per capita growth here means an annual increase of roughly $100 per person on the average, while a growth rate ten times higher in India would only increase incomes by about $30 per person. Clearly, to suggest an immediate narrowing of the gap in real terms would nourish a misleading hope.

We could, however, tip the *percentages* of growth in favor of poor countries. With respect to many developing countries that is already happening. Graph #5 shows that in recent years the rate of economic growth has been higher for developing countries as a whole than for industrialized countries. From 1960 to 1973 developing countries averaged a 6 percent growth rate, compared to 5 percent for industrial countries. From 1973 to 1982 the developing countries' rate of growth was almost double that of industrial countries (4.2 percent versus 2.1 percent). However, the higher rate of population growth in the developing countries (about 1.4 percent higher on average) effectively wiped out most of the growth rate advantages.

More disconcerting, the per capita growth rate for developing countries slipped substantially during the 1970's and in some instances

*Disposable personal income (after taxes) not adjusted for inflation. The real per capita U.S. income growth between 1973 and 1981, when adjusted for inflation, was about $510.

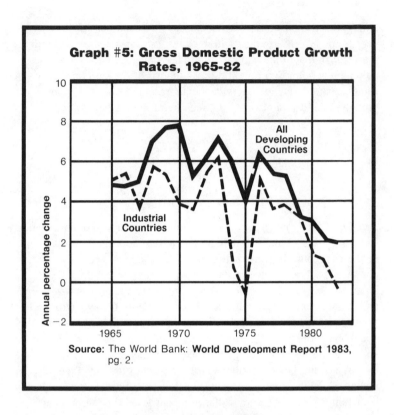

Graph #5: Gross Domestic Product Growth Rates, 1965-82

All Developing Countries

Industrial Countries

Annual percentage change

Source: The World Bank: **World Development Report 1983,** pg. 2.

went in reverse in the early 1980's as the worldwide recession swept over them. Still more alarming was the prospect that the long-term economic outlook for the developing countries would include higher inflation and slower growth than in the past. If so, barring major interventions, some of the poorest countries may have to choose between using scarce money either for development projects with a poverty focus or spending it on spare parts, fuel and food just to keep the economy floating. Either way, hunger is certain to flourish.

We need to distinguish between developing countries whose economic growth rate is relatively strong and those that are barely growing, if at all, on a per capita basis. Sixteen African countries, for example, have experienced an average annual *decrease* in per capita economic growth for more than a decade. And in 1983 the World Bank reported a real possibility that the per capita income of Africa's low-income countries, as a group, will be lower by the end of the 1980's than it was in 1960. In Africa and elsewhere the no-growth and slow-growth countries are those that, on the whole, have neither oil nor other compensating economic advantages that enable them to thrive.

As alarming as the income disparities *between* rich and poor nations is the fact that those disparities are usually evident *within* poor countries as well, where an affluent minority tends to absorb most of the gains. Rapid population growth can accelerate this trend by depressing wages through an oversupply of workers and by inflating land values and rents, as space becomes harder to secure. A widening income gap within developing countries can shrink already limited annual gains to pennies for the poor, and in some cases make them even poorer than before.

Despite the reality of hunger and poverty around the world and the astonishing gap between the "haves" and the "have nots," the past few decades have given rise to some dramatic gains, as well. Between 1960 and 1981 life expectancy in low-income developing countries increased from 41 to 58 years; and the proportion of infants surviving the first year of life increased from 84 percent to 90 percent in those countries during the same period. During 1960 and 1980 literacy increased from 39 percent to 56 percent of the adult population in developing countries. There are doubtless many factors that account for these gains, not the least of which is the ingenuity and dogged determination of people who, against the most discouraging obstacles, set out to make life better for themselves and others. These trends indicate that the forces of injustice are not the only ones at work. Stirring abroad are also signs of encouragement and hope. The slowing of economic growth in the 1970's and the ensuing recession also slowed, and in some countries may even have reversed, improvements in the physical quality of life, a worrisome development. Still, gains have been impressive.

The picture is mixed. The total number of poor and hungry people has probably been increasing, but the worldwide percentage of people living in hunger and absolute poverty has been declining. At best, the elimination of hunger will be a slow and exceedingly difficult task. Success will depend to a great extent on the availability of opportunities for the poorest billion people on earth. Their suffering sharpens Lester B. Pearson's warning that our planet cannot survive "half-slave, half-free, half-engulfed in misery, half-careening along toward the supposed joys of almost unlimited consumption.''[6]

We can play an important role in helping to provide those poorest billion people with opportunities so they can work their way out of hunger and poverty.

5
Environment, Resources and Growth

As the need to move swiftly and effectively against hunger increases, two new complications have surfaced: (1) the struggle for a clean environment; and (2) resource limitations. They affect both rich and poor nations, but pose special dilemmas for the poor ones, who find themselves facing additional handicaps when the deck has already been stacked heavily against them. Both dilemmas demonstrate that the struggle against hunger moves us inescapably to a quest for social justice.

Save the Environment: Two Movements

The campaign to save our environment mounts pressure against poor countries to pay an extra price as they industrialize: the cost of pollution control. For that matter, the pressure is felt on low income people in our own country and at times has surfaced in public clashes between those fighting for jobs and those fighting to conserve nature.

In reality *two* environmental campaigns are going on. One centers primarily on protecting nature and its ecosystems. The second concerns itself with social ecosystems that produce hunger, disease, and crowded hovels. By logic these two indispensable campaigns deserve to unite and strengthen each other. In practice they often collide.

The first campaign is being waged by those who are not so poor, some of whom are more indignant about smog than about slums, more worried about the mistreatment of animals and lakes than about mistreated people. This tends to pit the rights of nature against human rights. A higher passion for nature is not surprising, because most U.S.

citizens suffer from its abuse. Fewer of us are shorn of basics like food, shelter, medical care, work, income, and mobility.

In contrast, the second environmental struggle is prompted (if not always led) by those whose lives are battered by lack of these things. They have always struggled against nearly impossible odds, and now a new hurdle is being placed in their way. Another fee is being exacted. Rich people are upping the ante on them again. The poor of the world would probably like to breathe better air and keep their waterways pure, if they had decent jobs and enough to eat. But pollution-free hunger does not appeal to them.

In the United States the attempt to reverse environmental damage exacts a high price. Who pays the bill? All of us do, but barring clear measures toward assured employment and a more even distribution of incomes, the burden will continue to fall more heavily on those with low and moderate incomes. The wealthy may pay proportionately more but, unlike poor people, they do not need to worry that the fight for our natural surroundings will divert attention from *their* environment.

The conflict between nature-environmentalists and poverty-environmentalists is even more intense at the international level, with far greater stakes for the poor countries. The stakes are high, first of all, for them to keep nature in shape. A report by former UN Secretary-General U Thant, which prompted the United Nations to convene a world Conference on the Human Environment in Stockholm in 1972, itemized the horrors of failure, such as an estimated 1.25 billion acres of productive land lost through erosion or salt poisoning.

The stakes are also high in the cost of repairing or preventing damages. Consequently many poor nations feel saddled with the dilemma of having to choose between an immediate need to reduce poverty and a long-range need to preserve the environment—with pressure on them from us to prefer the latter. But if poor countries have to shoulder the whole burden of protecting their environment, when they are already struggling against hunger, they may understandably conclude that ''protecting the environment'' is another name for staying hungry.

Norman E. Borlaug, Nobel prize recipient for his work in the green revolution, has criticized ''irresponsible environmentalists'' who insist that DDT and related pesticides be banned from further use. The danger of DDT is widely known. It does not readily decompose, so its components are not recycled harmlessly into the earth. Instead it finds its way into the food chain and ultimately into human bodies in increasing (though as yet very minute) quantities. Borlaug asserted that this danger has been exaggerated and that a ban on DDT would mean increased hunger and starvation in the underdeveloped countries. The Food and Agriculture Organization also considers DDT and similar pesticides vital for food production in many countries and says that "until cheap, safe and efficient substitute pesticides are produced and made easily available, there is no alternative to the judicious use of DDT, especially in the developing world, to increase agricultural productivity to feed the growing number of people on our planet."

Are the environmentalists right in sounding an alarm on DDT? They probably are. While the extent of danger is subject to widely different interpretations, it would be foolish for us to take chances. DDT cannot be recalled like cars with faulty brakes. It enters the soil and water to stay—or to make its way into the food chain.

Are Borlaug and FAO right in arguing that such pesticides are vital to food production in the underdeveloped countries? Until effective alternatives appear, they are. What we have, then, is an impasse between urgent concerns that clash head on: one an immediate necessity, the other a long-range danger. If the past is any indication, immediate necessity will not be pushed aside. People who lack food will gladly take risks on DDT.

The above example is not an isolated one. The United Auto Workers sponsored a symposium in preparation for the 1972 UN conference at Stockholm. The symposium turned into a debate between youthful environmental enthusiasts and representatives of underdeveloped countries. "They say in Seoul, Korea, the smog is a mark of progress. It shows you're making it in American terms," complained a young Yale graduate. He had more to complain about. According to an ambassador from Sri Lanka, "Two-thirds of mankind, who live in the developing regions of the world, do not share the same concern about their environment . . . as the other one-third who live in the more affluent regions." He said that pure air, fresh water, and beauty would not be acceptable substitutes for economic progress. The delegate from Trinidad agreed. "I keep telling my colleagues that industrial pollution is not our problem, we would like to have more of it. . . ."[1]

Industrial pollution is the touchiest question, because poor nations are being asked to pay costs that the rich nations did not bother paying while they became rich. At Stockholm, after bitter debate on whether or not underdeveloped countries should receive some compensation for additional costs of environmental controls, the industrialized nations, led by the United States, voted no. The cost of controlling pollution amounts to a sizable new industrial tax. With underdeveloped countries severely pressed to industrialize faster, they can hardly be blamed for resisting a cost that makes industrial expansion more difficult. Of course, those countries must take care of their environment or incur debts for its neglect. At the same time they are under strong pressure to postpone payment—like we did—and concentrate now on economic development. That type of borrowing involves serious and uncertain risks for the world, but a "pay now, eat later" policy does not strike them as entirely fair.

The way to resolve this dilemma is to work it out on the basis of a unified world view. The logic of the natural environment, as well as the logic of human justice, calls us to deal not with separated parts but with the whole world. In that case the nature-environment and the poverty-environment movements will each have to adopt the cause of the other as part of its own.

But the main burden falls on the nature-environment people to humanize their outlook and campaign for human justice, because they can do so without the distraction of putting hungry children to bed. Otherwise, affluent people will certainly turn environmentalism into a self-serving and probably self-defeating enterprise. If the interdependence of life includes first and foremost the interdependence of people, then true environmentalism embraces freedom from hunger. That is the kind of movement on which both rich and poor nations need to unite.

Resource Limitations and Economic Growth

Although warning signs were on the horizon earlier, it was not until 1974, when the oil embargo, oil price hikes and global food shortages made their full impact, that the U.S. public came to realize that we could no longer take an almost unlimited supply of cheap natural resources for granted. Food prices went up here, while famine abroad provoked steady news coverage. The world's grain reserves dipped to the lowest point since the years immediately following World War II.

Oil prices, while grating to many of us, served notice that, except for new finds, known oil reserves could run dry within a matter of decades. One could hardly blame the otherwise impoverished Arab countries for getting what they can from a resource that might be theirs for a couple of generations at the present rate of consumption. The oil squeeze pushed this country to pursue alternate, costly and (especially in the case of nuclear power) controversial sources of energy.

Because manufactured nitrogen fertilizer, the chief commercial type, is a petroleum by-product, oil prices aggravated an already developing fertilizer shortage. Pesticides, as a derivative of crude oil, also became more expensive. Add land and water, the supply of which for expanding food production is limited, and you have, in the case of food, a striking example of a resource whose availability is related to the availability or scarcity of other resources, as well.

Food and energy are at stake, but so are other basic raw materials. Just as the food shortage led to the UN-sponsored World Food Conference in November 1974, so earlier that year the oil crisis prompted the United Nations to convene a special session of the General Assembly— not, however, merely on oil or energy, as the U.S. government hoped, but on raw materials in general. At this special session poor countries called for "a new international economic order" in which they would have adequate control over and fair prices for their raw materials, and assurance of long-range development opportunities.

Lester R. Brown has pointed out that in 1974 the United States was already dependent upon imports for more than half of its supply of six of the 13 basic raw materials required by a modern economy, and expects by the turn of the century to import most of its supply of all but one of the 13.

The question of supply limitations involves a wide range of resources and a great many uncertainties. For example, to what extent will additional reserves of oil be discovered, or alternate sources of energy developed? It is too early to say.

One thing is certain. The question of resource availability, following on the heels of the environmental movement, has pushed to the forefront a debate about economic growth. The outcome of this debate— measured not in oratory but in hardnosed decisions—will have far-reaching consequences for billions of present and future people who fall into the "hungry" column.

The limits-to-growth debate began in 1972 when interlocking problems—more people, limited resources, multiplying demand for them, increasing pollution—prompted an appeal strange to Western ears: restrain growth. In a document called *Blueprint for Survival,* 33 British citizens detailed a proposal for "a stable society"—that is, a society without economic or numerical growth. Two months later a group of scientists, sponsored by the Club of Rome, published *The Limits to Growth.* Using global data, they projected by a computerized "systems analysis" the distant consequences of continued growth. The starting assumptions fed into the computer were pessimistic on such things as the discovery and development of new resources, and the possibility of greatly reducing pollution—assumptions which rigged the outcome and brought heavy criticism ("Garbage in, garbage out," complained one critic.) Each model led ultimately to sudden collapse of growth either because of food or raw material shortages, or because of pollution. These scientists concluded that the only way to avoid an abrupt collapse would be to plan ahead for absolute limits on population, pollution, and production. That, they contended, means gradually halting economic growth.

Although the thesis that a nongrowing society offers the only alternative to ecological disaster has attracted a vocal following in this country, it has been adopted by relatively few scientists and is almost universally rejected in the poor countries. Global ecology is an infant science and its data still fragmentary. We know that the world's natural resources are not infinite. We hope to effectively harness solar energy and to make better use of additional raw materials, although estimating the extent to which we succeed at such efforts necessarily pushes us into guesswork.

Either a no-growth or a slow-growth future would create an enormous problem for the United States, but—as the worldwide recession of the early 1980's demonstrated—nothing like the crisis it would hand many poor countries. If there is to be a slow rate of growth, for example, how is that growth to occur? Would the rich nations limit their own consumption of raw materials so that the poor nations could process a larger share? Or would we lock the poor nations into starvation? That prospect is by no means remote, since most estimates concede that the earth's present population will soon double. If the rich nations *now* gobble up a lopsided share of new economic growth, then under conditions of *re-*

duced economic growth could poor nations look forward to getting even smaller portions for their swelling populations? Clearly, to propose a leveling off of growth raises the question of where that growth is to be concentrated. And that, in turn, pushes distribution of wealth to the forefront as an urgent issue.

The answer seems to lie in *more discriminately planned growth* in order to secure harmony with nature *and* justice for people. Such an approach postpones the question of the limits to growth, but it is the only effective way we have of working out an answer to that question. Meanwhile the assessment of the late Paul G. Hoffman, who once headed the UN Development Program, probably applies, that "increased productivity is necessary for providing both the financial and the technical resources to undo the environmental damage that has already been done."[2]

The heart of the matter for both rich and poor countries has to do more with the quality than with the quantity of growth. Nevertheless, the rate of growth makes a big difference. In 1979 the World Bank projected several hypothetical economic growth rates for the developing countries as a whole and estimated the impact of each on the number of persons who would be living in absolute poverty by the year 2000. By 1983 even the smallest of the projected growth rates looked optimistic, but the projections nevertheless show that the rate of growth cannot be ignored:

Annual Growth Rate	Persons in Absolute Poverty by 2000
4.8%	710 million
5.6%	600 million
6.6%	470 million

There is nothing sacred about these projections. They do not take into account, for example, that Brazil has a higher per capita income than Taiwan but, in proportion to the population, three times as many people living in absolute poverty. Changes in national policies can affect the outcome no matter what the rate of economic growth. On balance, however, it would be foolish to ignore the difference that the rate of growth is apt to make regarding the incidence of hunger and poverty in developing countries. The worldwide recession in the early 1980's clearly helped increase hunger and poverty in the United States, and it had an even more severe impact on developing countries. Thus the recession underscored the importance of growth and the relationships of growth to poverty.

Concentrating on the quality of growth may or may not slow the rate of growth. According to environmentalist Barry Commoner, "What happens to the environment depends on *how* the growth is achieved." By itself, halting economic growth could still be part of a formula for environmental disaster. As Commoner points out in *The Closing Circle,* the dramatic increase in U.S. environmental pollution since 1946 has occurred not primarily because of population growth or increased production, but because of new, pollution-intensive technologies which place unprecedented burdens on the life systems of nature. It is above all these technologies (for example, those involved in the production of synthetics such as plastics, fabrics, and pesticides) that have to be dealt with if we are going to make peace with our environment.

What kind of growth do we want? Should Detroit build more gas-guzzlers or durable economy cars and vehicles for mass transit? Should we base our decision on a surfeit of clever advertising that whets our appetites for products we do not need, in ever increasing amounts? Or can we concentrate on essentials and turn more of our labor force to service jobs that would improve our education, health services, parks and the like? We might be able to change a situation in which the United States, with 5 percent of the world's population, consumes about a third of the world's energy and minerals. We could have a growing economy that emphasizes improving the quality of life.

Style of Life

The five percent of the human race that lives in the United States produces and consumes more marketable wealth than do all the developing countries, with more than three-fourths of the world's population. This imbalance, along with concern for our stewardship of nature, has prompted many U.S. citizens to re-examine their style of living. The thrust, however modest, is toward a more sparing, less materialistic way of life.

The Christian tradition has valued (though Christians have not always practiced) simplicity of life and voluntary poverty, ideals drawn not least from Jesus himself, who had "nowhere to lay his head." It is expressed daily in the lives of millions of ordinary Christians, some with church-supported vocations, but most from the ranks of the laity. They have chosen to share what they have with others in response to the Gospel. The chief value of doing so is spiritual and symbolic—which is not to say "rather than real," as though spiritual and symbolic actions accomplish little. The transfer of resources involved is relatively limited. The power behind such commitment consists in lives that are placed more fully at the disposal of God and other people, and in keeping alive for others a sense of proportion.

Life-style adjustments should not, however, be viewed as a substitute for helping to enact needed public policies. Putting less fertilizer on your lawn and contributing the savings to a good cause may be useful for a variety of reasons, but in themselves these actions are congenial to the present hierarchy of wealth. They do not tinker with questions of justice. Regarding the environmental movement Barry Commoner writes: "What is just beginning to become apparent is that the debt [to nature] cannot be paid in recycled beer cans or in the penance of walking to work; it will need to be paid in the ancient coins of social justice—within nations and among them."[3]

Consider the example of energy. On a per capita basis we use almost twice the energy that West Germany does and almost three times that of Japan. A decade ago Peter G. Peterson, former Secretary of Commerce, reported that according to the Federal Energy Office this country wastes as much energy as Japan uses. Between 1973 and 1982, however, U.S. per capita energy consumption fell by 13 percent, due mainly to the combined impact of higher oil prices and a recession. Turning down our thermostats and driving less may have an integrity of their own, but they are not apt to make a big dent in energy waste. Substantial energy conservation is likely to come only as a result of economic pressure and/or national policy applied with the force of law. We need, then, to move from the personal to the public realm on such a matter, without abandoning personal efforts.

The waste of food in the United States suggests an almost endless list of ways in which we could conserve personally on this precious commodity. In 1983 U.S. citizens consumed an average of 1,725 pounds of grain, compared to an average of 400 pounds per person in poor countries, mainly beause we consumed most of ours indirectly as meat and dairy products. For example, the average pound of edible beef in this country represented about five pounds of grain in 1980, much of it consumed during the last few months on the feedlot, according to the National Cattlemen's Association. As a result the idea of "eating lower on the food chain" by cutting back on grain-fed meat makes sense during periods when the world supply of grain is tight and prices are high. But eating lower on the food chain does not automatically transfer food to hungry people. The grain "saved" may be sold to feed Russian livestock, induce farmers to plant less, or add to surplus stocks that prompt our government to subsidize their sale abroad at prices that undercut farmers in developing countries. Food will reach hungry people if government policies encourage its proper production and distribution; so an adjustment in eating habits without responsible citizenship may prescribe failure.

Adopting a more modest style of life can be a powerful witness in the struggle against hunger, if efforts to change public policy accompany it. Unfortunately many people attracted to a life-style approach want to stop there. Life-style changes appeal as immediate, personal responses. But they can also lull us with a false sense of fulfillment. Not having a television set because most people in the world do not have one, or riding a bicycle to work may be morally satisfying and bring personal benefits. Unless such actions are accompanied by other positive steps, however, they accomplish nothing for hungry people.

The appeal that is primarily needed is not for less personal consumption, but for a more positive national response to hunger. Therefore the most important sacrifice that readers of this book can make is the sacrifice of their time and energy to change public policy. Life-style adjustments are sorely needed, but detached from attempts to influence government policy they tend to be ineffective gestures. Our sense of stewardship must become sufficiently large to include both.

6
Up from Hunger

"Sir, I'm hungry!" pleaded a five-year old boy in Addis Ababa, Ethiopia.

He had approached Bernard Confer and Leslie Weber, both Lutheran executives engaged in world relief. They turned, and as Weber tells it, "I had no doubt about his being hungry. He wore a single cloth garment and his eyes bulged. I reached in my pocket and gave him a coin. Soon there were other children and my Ethiopian money was gone. My friend Confer commented, 'You have helped these children today, but who will help them tomorrow?' "

Who will help them tomorrow?

Or to ask the question underlying that one: How can we deal with the *causes* of hunger? What are its long-range remedies?

Because hunger springs from poverty, gains against hunger require development, the kind of development that enables people to climb above the most wretched forms of poverty.

The Development Struggle

Despite obstacles, seemingly unsurmountable at times, poor countries are not yet locked into despair. They still hope to work their way out of hunger, but doing so requires a combination of heroic effort on their part and greater cooperation on the part of other countries, including and especially our own.

Fortunately we are not starting from scratch. During the past four decades, while most of today's poor countries achieved their independence, a great range of development efforts took place. Results have been mixed, because the efforts were not always sufficiently wise or comprehensive; nevertheless, tens of millions have risen above the level of mal-nutrition and absolute poverty. They are the real measure of these efforts. In the process, nations and international agencies have worked together and accumulated a rich backlog of experience. Because the United States played a central role in opening a large flow of develop-ment assistance, we can find satisfaction in knowing that many more people would be hungry today without these initiatives.

In the process we have learned some of the things that work and some that do not. For example, we now know that a high rate of eco-nomic growth does not insure the kind of development that reaches the masses of poor people--although no one has figured out how develop-ment can occur among poor people without economic growth, either. During the decades of the 1960's and 1970's developing countries as a group averaged an increase in economic growth of more than five per-cent a year, a growth rate higher than that achieved by today's rich coun-tries, when they were in the earlier stages of development. Yet the gap between the "haves" and the "have-nots" widened and probably more people—though a smaller percentage of people—were poor at the close of the two decades than when they began.

Can we learn from this that development should occur primarily among the poor, and be measured less by the Gross National Product than by the quality of life? The world cannot contain five or ten billion persons consuming resources as rapidly as people in the United States do. But even if that were possible, would it be desirable? Christians who understand God's concern for the whole person and for the whole world should be especially conditioned to reach for a more human view of de-velopment, both here and abroad, not one that fastens mainly on income or production.

A country in which health services are available to all may be more highly developed than one with a more favorable ratio of physicians and hospitals, if these serve only the well-to-do. A country with beaches and parks for the public could be considered more advanced than one in which superior natural facilities are cornered by a minority of property owners. A country able to feed, house and employ its people adequately may be much better off than a wealthier country with a booming econ-omy and a wasteland of hunger. In short, development should be meas-ured primarily by what happens to people on the bottom half, not the top half, of the economy.

Efforts to develop along these lines meet with obstinate resistance, both from within poor countries and from elsewhere. One internal obstacle to development is *neglect of agriculture,* which will be examined more carefully later in this chapter. Another internal obstacle is *attachment to the status quo.* Persons with wealth or power to preserve, corrupt officials or merchants, or poor people who fail to understand the causes of poverty and passively accept their lot in life may all resist needed changes. A third is *poor allocation of resources*—in capital-intensive industry, for example, when capital is scarce and labor abundant; in show-case development projects; or in excessive military spending. Other internal obstacles may stem from the period of colonialism, when systems of education, communications, transportation, commerce and even food production were created for the purpose of exporting cheap raw materials or cash crops to the controlling country, not for local development. To reflect even a bit on these obstructions is to realize how difficult it is to overcome them.

Not all obstacles to development lie within the poor nations, however. Many are still imposed on them by the rich countries. These external obstacles, which also reflect the reluctance of those with advantages to give them up, include: (1) trade and investment practices that stack the deck against poor countries; (2) scarcity of genuine development assistance; and (3) "cultural colonialism" by which rich nations impose on poor countries growth-distorting values or systems—schools that prepare a few for college, but leave the rest ill-equipped to be better farmers or workers; or advertising that develops a craving for luxury products, from Cokes to cars, rather than for basic commodities.

These obstacles to development threaten to bury the poor world in a permanent sea of misery. They have to be dealt with candidly by both rich and poor nations through the adoption of positive alternatives. For this reason I will sketch an approach to development that begins where most hungry people still live: on the countryside.

Accent on Agriculture

The elimination of hunger calls for economic growth that is equitable, self-reliant and environmentally sound, with emphasis on a strong agricultural base and the maximum employment of labor.

Equitable growth implies some semblance of fairness. Whether 50 or 15 percent of the population lives in poverty, the goal of equitable growth requires at the very least that gains in the economy not bypass the poor, but rather enable them to contribute their abilities and participate fully in the benefits of those gains.

Self-reliant growth applies both to a nation and to the people within it. Self-reliance does not conflict with healthy interdependence. But it does mean that individuals as well as countries should use their own resources and ingenuity to the utmost. They may need assistance in order to develop those resources, but they should avoid inordinate and prolonged dependence on others. For developing countries ''others'' could mean other countries, financial institutions or multi-national corporations, excessive dependence on which is apt to skew their development efforts away from the meeting of basic human needs. Because individuals overwhelmingly desire opportunity and dignity, self-reliance has enormous appeal. Joe Short, former executive director of Oxfam-America, reports that when Oxfam was distributing food rations in Cambodia during its famine, hundreds of people waited quietly for their share; but when fish nets were handed out, the crowd cheered.

Environmentally sound growth means growth that utilizes but does not violate natural resources. Failure to live in harmony with nature invites eventual hardship. For example, the plowing of marginal land below the Sahara Desert has been slowly turning more land into desert.

Economic growth should build a strong agricultural base. Much of the world goes hungry because farmers and farm workers are a neglected majority. In underdeveloped countries three-fourths of the population, including the vast majority of the world's poor and hungry people, live off the land. To reverse a saying of Jesus: the laborers are plentiful but the harvest is few.

One good result that emerged from the famines of the 1970's was the turning of attention to agriculture, where a revolution of attitudes, changes in practice, and many more resources are needed. Although the World Food Conference set impressive goals toward bringing about such a revolution, progress has been disappointingly slow.

Farmers living on a subsistence level or barely above it understandably resist change, when one miscalculation can destroy the thin security which their traditional habits insure. Paul E. Johnson, former Operations Division Chief of the Office of Food for Peace, relates this experience:

> When I was in Afghanistan 15 years ago, we tried to get the farmers to advance from the sickle to the scythe. A team of three Austrians worked at it for four years; a very capable young Swiss farm-tools technician with FAO spent two years on the project. After all this the Afghan farmer continued to use the sickle. Using the scythe he could cut as much wheat in an hour as he could cut with the sickle in 3 or 4, but the scythe shattered more of the grain and reduced his net yield slightly. With only an acre or two of land and with wife and children to help him in the field, labor costs were not important, but each teacup full of wheat was important in feeding hungry mouths until the next harvest.[1]

No matter how much he may want to better himself, a farmer eking out a marginal existence cannot afford to gamble. Improvements have to be demonstrated, and must be part of an integrated program of change that offers him a social and economic security more dependable than the one he is asked to give up. The eagerness with which farmers grabbed hold of "green revolution" technologies shows, however, that given clear opportunity for improving their conditions, farmers adopt new methods as readily as anyone else. That some abandoned those technologies in 1974, when shortages and costs drove them out of reach, underlines the need of farmers for security.

Improvements can give a farmer pride in himself and in his vocation. As of now, most countries suffer at every level from a bias against agriculture, and ambitions are directed away from rather than toward it. Speaking about this, agriculturalist Norman Borlaug says, "The miseries of life on the land are such that once you get an education you want to become a doctor or a lawyer or professor—anything but an agricultural scientist."[2] This attitude toward agriculture has become institutionalized by leaders in government, business, and the professions, who feel exactly the same way about farm work as the peasants do. "The agricultural adviser should be the main instigator of technical progress," writes René Dumont in *The Hungry Future*. "But in Africa he is a comparatively underestimated official and all he wants is a position in the capital, after a period in Europe. He is not nearly so well treated as his colleagues in the Health and Education Departments.''[3] Dumont reports an experience with an Asian agricultural adviser who refused to go into the rice fields, in order to keep his shoes from getting muddy.

Poor countries need a national goal for rural improvement and an idealism that prompts workers with a broad range of skills to go to farms and villages to involve rural people in development.

Swiftly climbing unemployment explains in part why rural development must get urgent attention. Driven by hunger and poverty on the countryside, and lured by visions of a better life, millions flow to the cities each year looking for jobs. Too often the jobs aren't there. Families settle in shantytowns, and if unemployment persists, broken homes, alcoholism and crime may follow. In the poor countries urbanization is taking place at a far more rapid rate than it ever did in Europe or the United States. Once again today's poor are ''getting there too late''—at a time when industry tends to move toward high-cost, labor-saving technology. To find something like it in the United States you turn to the migration from the rural South of several million impoverished blacks, who arrived in the cities when unskilled hands were no longer in demand. Because our situation has never been honestly faced, it has generated difficulties far out of proportion to the original problem. Still, it is microscopic compared to the migration now going on in the underdeveloped countries.

The rising demand for food and employment, plus the fact that most hungry people live on the countryside suggest these steps:

1. *A labor-intensive approach to agriculture.* Poor countries *do* have people who need work. They do *not* have capital to buy machinery that is not essential. It makes sense for them to utilize what they have, not what they lack. Fortunately most improvements toward higher production, such as higher-yield seeds, fertilizer, irrigation, second-cropping, terracing, improved plowing and weeding, and harvesting higher yields, require mainly additional labor. More labor is also necessary for roads, storage and supply centers, schools, clinics, and a host of other improvements. The evidence is abundantly clear that small-scale, labor-intensive farming can usually bring higher yields per acre than large-scale, mechanized farming.

2. *Land reform*. In many poor countries, farm families own little or no land and have neither the means nor the incentive to increase production. The situation varies from area to area. In India, farms have either gotten larger through mechanization or been carved into smaller and smaller units under the crush of population growth. Either process creates more landless workers who are often serfs in lifelong debt to their landlord. In Latin America, owners of huge estates seldom invest their profits in rural development, and what little the governments get from them in taxes seldom goes there, either. Millions are left without hope or incentive.

If land reform is essential for development in so many countries, why is it so widely ignored? Because prosperous landowners don't like it. Imagine the resistance in our own country to a movement for chopping up corporate farms or Southern plantations into smaller family units. Conservative leaders in Latin America chafed when President Kennedy had land reform written into the principles of the Alliance for Progress in 1961. They ignored it, and after Kennedy's death, land reform dropped from the language of U.S. officials as well. Ironically it surfaced again almost two decades later as a hastily conceived measure to undercut the appeal of revolutionaries in El Salvador, when that country became vulnerable to a leftist takeover. But when a right-wing government was elected in El Salvador, land reform stalled.

3. *Industrial development that is related to rural development*. The tendency has been to forget agriculture and develop industries. It hasn't worked. But putting industry to work for agriculture, and vice versa, spreads gains throughout the entire population. For example, industry can concentrate on manufacturing fertilizer, tools, and other products vital to farming. Industry can also develop along labor-intensive lines. Much of it can be located in rural centers for turning out basic products, such as clothing and furniture, that use mainly local materials and local skills.

The experience of the West during the Industrial Revolution deserves emphasis. It is ironic that people in the underdeveloped countries who want to copy Western industrial patterns tend to downgrade agriculture, overlooking the fact that integration of industry and agriculture was central to development in the West. Initial stages of industrial growth in Europe and North America depended upon earlier agricultural development, and as farmers became consumers, they helped to spawn industries not directly related to agriculture. Today, as well, countries need agricultural development as a base for industrial growth. There are exceptions, of course. Singapore and Saudi Arabia will presumably never have a strong agricultural base. But these exceptions do not detract from the rule.

What are the consequences of slighting agriculture and neglecting rural life? Doing so hinders food production and distribution. It insures that the income gap will continue to widen in most developing countries. It stimulates migration from farms to cities, transferring unemployment and poverty to places where they are even more difficult to cope with. If the world's hungry are to eat well, and if development is to have meaning for more than a privileged minority, then the overall strategy of emphasizing agriculture makes sense.

Participation and Power

One of the underlying causes of hunger and poverty is the view held by many that poor people are victims of fate and there is little or nothing they can do to change their lot in life (analogous to "You can't fight city hall"). Although this viewpoint is losing adherents, it is still widespread. The view is not irrational. It is rooted in extensive personal and collective suffering that over the centuries has produced a sense of powerlessness. As long as impoverished people look at life fatalistically or are prevented by others from taking steps that would enable them to improve their circumstances, they will remain powerless—and poor.

Non-poor people need to begin removing some of the obstacles that lock others into hunger and poverty. And many who are mired in hunger and poverty need to begin thinking differently about themselves, their surroundings and possible opportunities. This changing awareness can and should take place with the encouragement of a government which, as the central characteristic of its development policy, sees its people as the nation's most valued resource, the end as well as the means of development. But real participation of the poor in their development involves an active role for them in making decisions about their own and their nation's future. That kind of participation begins to shift some economic and political power toward them. Inescapably, those who have an economic or political stake in keeping things as they are will find such a shift threatening. Consequently, participation by the poor seldom comes about without controversy or struggle. However, it does not have to be understood in terms of an ideology or associated with revolution. In fact, revolution has little appeal to poor people who are able to improve their lives through peaceful development.

As an example of such participation, consider some tribal villages near Calcutta that a few years ago were gradually becoming small centers of production. Villagers had started cottage industries. They were also turning barren land into small productive plots by building irrigation systems. Next to one village was a huge reservoir that villagers had dug with hand tools as part of a food-for-work project. Villagers spoke of a nearby landowner who owned more land than was legally permitted and who also served as the local money lender. He tried, by promising them water, to discourage them from digging the reservoir. They all owed him money. When asked how much interest he charged, they replied by citing bags of rice and days of labor, translated into annual interest rates ranging from 200 to 300 percent. Digging that reservoir and bringing barren land into production was a way of getting out from under the moneylender and moving up to an improved level of nutrition and poverty. In the process they were also developing new self-esteem and modest economic leverage, as well as a stronger sense of community.

Drawing on several decades of experience in development by donor countries, Rutherford M. Poats in his 1983 report as chairman of the 17-nation Development Assistance Committee drew this conclusion regarding development in predominantly agricultural low-income countries: "The key lesson has been that the reduction of poverty and its shadow, hunger, in such countries depends in the long run upon the broadening of popular participation in economic growth, especially agriculture-based growth."[4]

Models of Development

Efforts to develop show widespread diversity. No two countries are alike, and the great majority of poor nations avoid lining up in the camp of either communist-type socialism or unrestrained capitalism. Most try to find their own path, with practical considerations playing a much bigger role than economic theories.

In Latin America Brazil stood out for years as an "economic miracle" with an annual growth rate of 10 percent for seven consecutive years, from 1968 to 1974. But Brazil's Minister of Finance said candidly in 1972 that only five percent of the population had benefitted from the country's economic growth, and that same year *The Wall Street Journal* reported that most of Brazil's people were as poor or poorer than when the boom began. According to a 1974 analysis, unchallenged by the Brazilian government, the real purchasing power of the bottom two-thirds of the population had fallen sharply over a ten-year period. Economic growth slowed in the late 1970's and by 1983 Brazil had experienced three years of economic decline. Brazil reflects a guided but relatively unrestrained type of capitalism that by 1983 had operated for two decades under military dictators but was returning to democracy. Few if any countries have such an extreme disparity in incomes as does Brazil. In 1972 the lowest 20 percent of households earned two percent of the income, and the highest 20 percent earned 67 percent—more than 33 times the income of the poorest 20 percent.

Cuba, the Latin American version of communism, has wiped out hunger and unemployment. It has lifted its farm workers out of dismal poverty and offers health care, education and economic security to all citizens. Food and other products are severely rationed, and absenteeism from work and school runs high—a phenomenon unheard of in China. In 1980 Cuba received $3 billion in economic aid from the Soviet Union, approximately 25 percent of Cuba's total economic output—an astonishing dependency. Civil liberties are severely limited in this totalitarian regime.

Chile, traditionally one of the most prosperous and democratic countries in Latin America, found itself with a duly-elected Marxist president in 1970. Salvador Allende won a plurality, but not a majority of the votes in a three-way contest. Allende tried to help Chile's poor to substantial improvements; but high inflation, opposition from the middle and upper classes, and other factors (some would include political ineptitude or outside pressures) led to Allende's overthrow. A hard-line military regime seized power in September 1973 and brought both stability and a recession that spurred hunger and unemployment. In 1975 General Pinochet installed a stricter free market economy. Between 1977 and 1981 the economy grew at an annual rate of 8.5 percent and was hailed as another "miracle." Then in 1982 the economy plunged by 14 percent into a depression, unemployment soared, and by late 1983 Pinochet's government appeared to be tottering.

In Africa Kenya and Tanzania, neighbors on the eastern coast, illustrate different approaches to development on that continent.

Kenya, endowed with more abundant natural resources, chose capitalism, welcomed most foreign investments, and during the first decade following independence in 1963 saw its economy grow at the average rate of 6.5 percent annually. Its agricultural growth rate was lower but impressive at 4.7 percent. Health and literacy gains were dramatic. So was the population growth rate, which eventually reached 4 percent. In the early 1970's the economy slowed down. Studies showed that 30 percent of the population was living in poverty, with poverty measured by nutrition-based income needs. A survey revealed that the benefits of Kenya's growth had bypassed most of the rural population, which is to say most Kenyans. A new strategy in the early 1980's began to remove protections and subsidies on industries and to favor a freer market. Food prices were raised to give farmers more income and incentive to produce. The strategy also aimed more health, education, nutrition and family planning services to rural areas. But the world recession, depressed prices for tea and coffee (Kenya's main exports), mounting unemployment and rising debts clouded the horizon for Kenya in the early 1980's.

Tanzania, the poorer of the two countries, with an annual per capita income of $280 in 1981, is attempting to carve out a distinctively African type of socialism. President Julius Nyerere lives in a simple house and is committed to a type of development in which all participate and benefit on a relatively equal basis. His government has sought to turn villages into cooperatives based on the tribal custom of communally held land. However, management problems and the resistance of villagers to communal farming have greatly frustrated these efforts. In recent years Tanzania was severely hit by worldwide recession, oil price hikes and worsening terms of trade. The resulting shortages of oil, spare parts and supplies crippled the economy and further hampered efforts at the village level. Recurring drought conditions have contributed to a decline in per capita food production. Despite extensive outside assistance, Tanzania's future looked bleak in the early 1980's.

In Asia, Japan became a rich, developed nation while most of today's poor countries were still colonies. It has special advantages: a non-tropical climate and social cohesion that helped Japan fend off attempts by the West to make it a colony. Drastic reforms, including land reform, paved the way for industrial growth, and Japan achieved a kind of national partnership in which government, banking, industry and labor work together: a benevolent capitalistic version of central planning. Diligence and a literacy rate higher than our own are two of Japan's assets, but this country's weakness lies in heavy dependence on imports of oil, food and other raw materials. With very limited natural resources, Japan lays great emphasis on technological excellence and massive exports. Despite its unique situation, Japan provides some encouragement for developing countries with limited natural resources.

China concentrated on modern industry in the 1950's and millions streamed to the cities to find neither jobs nor housing—a familiar story. Then in a major policy switch China decided to wrap its development efforts around agriculture and allied industries, with some success, despite abhorrent excesses of the Cultural Revolution. Now more than one billion Chinese, with an annual per capita income in 1983 of roughly $300, are moving toward modernization largely unassisted.

Our knowledge of China is still much too limited. Visits by specialists since 1971 reveal impressive gains. *Life* correspondent John Saar noted a level of overall poverty but saw "no hunger, no untreated sick, no beggars"—an observation verified by others. Gone, too, are the prostitutes and opium smokers. Swollen eyes and open skin sores no longer plague the peasants. City, streets and villages are immaculate. Unemployment has been greatly reduced, though not eliminated. If wages are meager, everyone is assured housing, education, medical care and food, although the supply is not always adequate. Today China is moving forward with determination against enormous obstacles. The world has never before witnessed an attempt on such a scale to build and sustain a new society from bottom up. However, the glowingly one-sided reports about China that characterized the early 1970's have been discredited. Much was wrong with China's economy, among other things—though the problems were cleverly disguised—and in the early 1980's China's leaders were attempting to increase farm and industrial output by, of all things, instituting profit incentives and encouraging private enterprise on a limited scale, including private foreign companies.

China's experiment shows a passionate totalitarianism that harbors little dissent. With a highly centralized, authoritarian government, China has the ability to industrialize with some speed through "forced savings"—in a manner not altogether unlike that of the capitalists of the Industrial Revolution in the nineteenth and early twentieth centuries, who extracted enormous profits from the sweat of the workers, profits they kept investing in more industrial expansion. Even so, this kind of go-it-alone development presupposes mineral resources needed for industrialization, and a great variety of skilled technologists—conditions few other countries enjoy.

The Chinese model is one of repulsion-attraction to the rest of the underdeveloped world. Its harsh regimentation repels, but the Chinese have to arrange life with perhaps one-thirtieth of the per capita wealth that we enjoy.

India's plight can be quickly illustrated: almost as many people as Africa and South America combined, an annual per capita income of about $260, and tens of millions unemployed in the cities. Nearly half of the population lives below the official poverty line, which in India is not much more than a starvation line. The caste system (illegal but alive) and other traditions, including a diversity of languages, make development difficult. India's blend of free enterprise and socialism has not always worked well, though economic theory may have little to do with that. Despite these and other deficiencies, India remains a relatively strong democracy and has shown resilience and capacity for modest growth, with a 1.4 percent average annual GNP growth rate per person between 1960 and 1981. India has also become self-reliant in food production in the sense that it no longer is a net importer of grain except in years of widespread drought. About 10 percent of the population has risen to a middle class economic level. A question hotly debated is whether this middle class is part of a rising tide that will eventually lift all the boats or is leaving the other boats stranded.

A "New Economic Order"?

What kind of world do we want to help build, not just in the fantasy of idle dreams, but with personal efforts? If we seek a world in which even the poor are able to work and eat and live on at least a minimally decent level, a world that in the long run has a reasonable chance of holding together with its humanity intact, then a greatly expanded program for development makes sense. At best this will be a long, hard struggle stretching well beyond our lifetimes. And it will mean making sizable accommodations to poor countries without delay.

Poor countries, too, are asking: What kind of world do we want to build? They, through considerable hardship, also see the need for accommodation on our part. To them it is a matter of simple justice. Understandably they are no longer waiting passively for rich nations to take the initiative. They are bringing their case to the court of world opinion, in public forums such as the United Nations, and using economic leverage where they have it. As oil showed, for some countries the leverage lies in their raw materials, which industrialized nations depend upon.

The UN General Assembly's special session on raw materials in April 1975 issued a declaration for "a new international economic order." Backed primarily by the poor countries, the declaration seeks a system that would assure them of (1) control of their own natural resources, (2) fair prices and open markets for their exports, (3) increased development assistance free of political or military conditions, and (4) an adequate flow of resources for their development. Included in the last item is reform of the monetary system so that more international credit reserves are allocated to developing countries.

These proposals are not unreasonable, though reaching agreement on specific steps to implement them will not be easy, as a decade of studied rejection by the rich northern countries demonstrated. By the early 1980's a world recession made their achievement seem even more remote. But the prosperous countries might well have pursued them years earlier, had they placed the ending of hunger seriously on their agendas.

The fact that all countries—rich, poor and in between—have a huge stake in a better world economy could set the stage for agreements to achieve it. Doing so will take a combination of pushing on the part of poor countries and willingness to make concessions on the part of our own and other affluent countries. The cost to us would not be small. But what kind of future, what judgment of God, do we invite if we fail to move in this direction?

The Gospel and Human Justice

Concern for human justice may seem to many to be far afield from the Gospel of Christ. Not at all. What prompts Christians to respond to others is God's love and visible human need. God's love sets us free to care deeply about others, so when their need confronts us, we act. But if our faith and love are genuine, we will want that action to do more than make us feel good or bestow temporary relief. We will want our action to deal with their need as effectively as possible. Dealing effectively with hunger clearly pushes us into the public policy arena, into questions of social justice.

Grounding our ethic in the Gospel, we affirm for others a right that we enjoy: the right to food. We want the hungry to overcome a situation that flagrantly violates their humanity. To see them not secretly as inferiors, but truly as brothers and sisters of the same heavenly Father, is to earnestly desire their full human dignity as his children. Christian concern, then, precisely because it springs from the Gospel, moves us to seek the justice that God invites us to celebrate.

Part III

The Need for a U.S. Commitment on Hunger

7
The Rediscovery of America

The United States is a great country and a generous country, but we have drifted away from our own tradition of generosity. As a nation we are not seriously trying to help the human race overcome hunger. We have no vision for joining with poor countries to arrange a more livable world.

Retreat from a Hungry World

The vision is not beyond reach. It has occasionally been sketched by our leaders, but for more than two decades they have studiously avoided summoning the nation to act on any such vision. Secretary of State Henry A. Kissinger provided two striking examples in 1974. At the UN Special Assembly on Raw Materials, in April, he told the world:

> On behalf of President Nixon, I pledge the United States
> to a major effort in support of development. My country ded-
> icates itself to this enterprise because our children, yours and
> ours, must not live in a world of brutal inequality.

"We are part of a large community," he said, "in which wealth is an obligation, resources are a trust, and joint action is a necessity." The words appeared to signal a major initiative by the United States, but no such initiative came. We continued to pursue policies that, for example, left us near the bottom among donor countries, when development assistance is measured as a percentage of national production.

In November 1974 at the World Food Conference in Rome, Kissinger proposed the goal "that within a decade no child will go to bed hungry," and urged joint action "to regain control over our shared destiny.

If we do not act boldly, disaster will result from a failure of will.'' But a decade later—and despite reports on world hunger commissioned by Presidents Ford and Carter—bold action was noticeably absent. In 1984 UNICEF reported that more than 40,000 young children died *each day* from malnutrition and infection.

The Role of U.S. Ideals

This retreat from the world of hunger has been accompanied for several decades by the enlargement of U.S. military power. *But the strength of the nation lies more in its ideals, and in the practice of those ideals, than in the flexing of national muscles.* Put another way, power is nothing new. The world has seen power as long as nations have existed, sometimes trembling before it, sometimes submitting to it, but never loving it. Others have loved the United States, but seldom for its power. Rather what captured the admiration of people throughout the world was the fact that, for all its faults and contradictions, this country wrested its independence from England and started a new experiment in freedom. In setting out the nation's course, its founding leaders declared that ''all men are created equal,'' and they determined to shape the nation's destiny along democratic lines.

To invoke national ideals is not to deny fundamental departures. Freedom from the colonists and pioneers also meant freedom to seize land from the Indians, and to make slaves or second-class citizens of black people. These violations of human dignity have left ugly and abiding scars, and they continue to be a contributing cause of hunger. But at least it is possible to recognize them as contradictions to be resolved, because they fail to harmonize with the principles upon which the nation was established.

Those who settled in our land came with no unified set of principles. They were dissenters, religious refugees, acquisitive people, adventurers, people fleeing depression and famine, fugitives from justice, rich and poor people, good and bad. They represented a host of national and cultural backgrounds. But they made this a country where freedom and democracy were celebrated, if not always honored in practice. The United States of America was more than a new nation. It became a *movement* rooted in equality, and embodying the hope of "liberty and justice for all."

The terms liberty, justice and equality have deep biblical roots. When applied by a nation they do not deal with the relationship between God and his human creatures, but they do draw heavily from the implications of that relationship and from the biblical view of the Kingdom, and therefore they are ideals that Christians and Jews have special reason to cherish.

The lessons of the nation's past tell us that liberty and justice cannot be secured for ourselves and kept from others without turning sour. Because we have cherished liberty for others, this country has sacrificed enormously (if not always wisely) in lives and material resources. We have not cherished justice as much. But justice and equality are no less a part of the nation's ideals, and we build on them by exercising them in our relationship with others. When we are rich and others are hungry or impoverished beyond description, justice calls for ending this imbalance.

Strength Versus Power

Internally and internationally, the strength of our nation lies in its ideals. Without them we are like Samson shorn of his hair. Unfortunately we have relied increasingly on raw power. Contrary to some critics, the shift toward power was not cynical. In part the circumstances of history thrust it upon us, and in part it grew out of a misunderstanding. Until the end of World War II, much of the poor world knew the United States as the champion of self-determination. To many we were heroes. We stood for an end to colonialism and for freedom to the colonies, despite some colonial adventures of our own. After World War II a new factor emerged—the extension of communist domination over Eastern Europe and success of the communists of China. The communist takeover in Eastern Europe and the threat of similar developments in Greece and Turkey were reviewed with alarm as a new form of colonialism, and as such prompted a vigorous military build-up under our sponsorship, beginning with the NATO countries of Western Europe.

This militant anticommunist stance took place as the *continuation* of our opposition to colonialism. But it locked us into an oversimplified interpretation. The communist revolution in China, for example, did not turn out to be part of a Soviet conquest, but a nationalist uprising with hard-line Marxist ideas. In fact the Soviet Union reacted to "losing" China far more intemperately than we did. (We vilified our China experts, Stalin executed his.) The same oversimplified interpretation, however well motivated, prevented us from understanding Vietnam and led to the tragedy of military intervention there.

Vietnam can only be understood against a century-long background of colonialism. Like most of today's underdeveloped world, Indochina was gobbled up by a European power. France, anxious for the grandeur of empire, forced its way into Vietnam in 1857 and fought for decades to control Indochina. Armed resistance never disappeared in that colony. The Vietnamese, unified somewhat by language and by a long history of opposition to Chinese invaders, drew strength from a nationalism already well established.

Under France, the gap between rich and poor widened. In *Asian Drama* Gunnar Myrdal reports:

> The Vietnamese were generally excluded from the modern sectors of their economy as well as from higher posts in the government. Banking, mining, large-scale manufacturing industry, and rubber production were jealously guarded French preserves. . . .In addition, French settlers, usually of peasant stock and with a background of service in the lower ranks of the French army, acquired large amounts of land. . . .[1]

Myrdal also found that "Frenchmen of lower-class origin" occupied positions in government and business for which, by contrast, the British in India trained Indians. This practice of the French excluded the Indochinese still more.

France fought movements toward eventual self-rule, so moderate nationalism had no chance to emerge in Vietnam. France prohibited political parties and trade unions. The consequence, writes Myrdal, "was to leave the underground Communist Party in the forefront of the Vietnamese struggle for independence." The French, who in effect recruited for the communist movement, could claim that in fighting Vietnamese nationalists they were fighting communism.

President Roosevelt wanted France out and Indochina independent, much to De Gaulle's displeasure. In 1944 Roosevelt wrote to Cordell Hull:

> France has had the country—thirty million inhabitants—for nearly one hundred years, and the people are worse off than they were at the beginning. . . . France has milked it for one hundred years. The people of Indochina are entitled to something better than that.[2]

In 1947 Secretary of State George C. Marshall advised France to make peace with Ho Chi Minh on generous terms, and warned that continuing the war or attempting to set up a puppet government might play into the hands of communists throughout Asia by putting democracies in a bad light. Despite this warning, the United States began to support French colonialism once more, paying for 80 percent of France's war by 1954 and then finally—as far as the Vietnamese understood it—replacing France as the colonial power.

One reason we misread Vietnam, ironically, is that our record of colonial rule (in the Philippines, for example) was benevolent compared with that of the French. As a result we failed to understand the intense feeling of the Vietnamese against foreign intervention, or why our intervention, so well intended in the eyes of most of us, should meet with such hostility. So instead of encountering a situation analogous to Korea, in Vietnam we reaped the consequences of a century of French misrule and found ourselves defending corrupt regimes that had little popular support.

Vietnam illustrates, rather than contradicts, the fact that our military commitments abroad and the enormous sacrifices these entailed were motivated primarily by a desire to prevent another colonial power (or powers) from gobbling up helpless countries. In the process, however, the United States has placed itself in the unpopular role of world policeman, accused of practicing the colonialism we sought to prevent. Because that role involves a shift away from influence by example and toward influence by power, it obscures our ideals, and in the long run undermines our purposes.

The use of the struggle against communism as our primary tool for measuring situations abroad is a mistake for several reasons. It is a negative approach; we define ourselves by what we are *against* rather than by what we are *for*. That distorts. We cannot base a convincing program on our ideals and project it to the world by stressing what we oppose.

The approach is also based on fear. It shows an excessive awe of communism and too little confidence in democracy. We must be realistic and recognize the threat which the communist mixture of totalitarianism and idealism still represents. We cannot ignore what happened to Hungary, Czechoslovakia and Afghanistan. But the facts fail to support a position of abject fear, of mental paralysis. Do not setbacks to communism during the past two decades in many poor countries, because of domestic reactions against it, dispel the myth of communist invincibility? Do not fundamental splits between communist countries likewise lay to rest the phantom of a unified international movement against us?

In addition this negative approach is wrong because the problems that communism depends upon for winning converts—hunger, poverty, repression—are successfully attacked not with guns, but with social reforms and economic gains.

Our preoccupation with anticommunism has also moved us toward the support of too many totalitarian regimes, a stance that clearly violates the ideals we want to promote. To talk about ideals is not enough. Echoing President Johnson on Vietnam, President Nixon assured the nation that we were "only fighting for the right of people far away to choose the kind of government they want." But the runner-up to President Thieu in South Vietnam's 1967 election was in prison; and Thieu's one-man contest in 1971, followed by various repressive actions, showed that nothing of the sort was happening in Saigon. Further, while Nixon spoke, the United States was shipping arms to the Pakistani government, which was engaged in savage repression of the people of East Pakistan (now Bangladesh), who *had* expressed their will in contested elections. We cannot expect developing nations to be immediate, mature, full-blown democracies; but our policies should encourage a free expression by the people in any country.

Greece, the birthplace of democracy, is another case in point. In 1967 a group of army colonels seized power, suspended constitutional rights and shut down parliament. A thousand-page report by the 15 nations of the Council of Europe, which later expelled Greece from the Council, documented cases of brutality and torture. Washington, however, ignored the Council and in 1970 resumed full shipment of heavy arms to Greece. Business, as well as the government, was implicated when in April of 1971 Secretary of Commerce Maurice H. Stans spoke in Athens before high-ranking government officials:

> We in the United States government, particularly in American business, greatly appreciate Greece's attitude toward American investment, and we appreciate the welcome that is given here to American companies and the sense of security that the government of Greece is imparting to them.[3]

Overthrow of the Greek military leaders in 1974 left the United States widely discredited in Greece, as democratic elements regained control.

The case of Iran is even starker. For years we poured billions of dollars into that country to shore up the military regime of the Shah, because we saw him as a dependable ally against communism. But a popular uprising ousted the Shah and 52 U.S. Embassy personnel were held hostage for 444 days in an expression of outrage against the United States, which was widely blamed for the injustices that abounded under the Shah. Did those billions of dollars bring us more security and respect? To ask the question is to know the answer.

Too much reliance on power, coupled with fear of communism, has even led us to take part in misguided military interventions. Vietnam is not the only example. The year 1961 found us deeply involved in the Bay of Pigs fiasco in Cuba. In 1965 the U.S. Marines invaded the Dominican Republic to dismantle a reformist revolution that had seized power. Regarding that, former Senator J. William Fulbright has written:

> The central fact about the intervention of the United States in the Dominican Republic was that we had closed our minds to the causes and to the essential legitimacy of revolution in a country in which democratic procedures had failed. The involvement of an undetermined number of communists in the Dominican Revolution was judged to discredit the entire reformist movement, like poison in a well, and rather than use our considerable resources to compete with the communists for influence with the democratic forces who actively solicited our support, we intervened militarily on the side of a corrupt and reactionary military oligarchy. We thus lent credence to

the idea that the United States is the enemy of social revolution, and therefore the enemy of social justice, in Latin America.[4]

Anti-communism as the guiding star of our foreign policy leads us
to positions that are foolish when measured by traditional U.S. ideals.
Consider, for example, our "tilt" toward Pakistan in 1971 because of its
militant anti-communism. After the Pakistani army had for eight months
committed crimes that forced ten million Bengalis to flee into India,
President Nixon publicly commended that country's ruler, then General
Yahya Khan, for his efforts "to reduce tensions in the subcontinent."
Meanwhile an even more astonishing example was shaping up in Chile.

In 1970 Chile elected by plurality a Marxist president—a distaste-
ful outcome for many U.S. citizens. The fact remains that Salvador Allende was elected through the democratic process by the voters of Chile.
After his election the United States used the Central Intelligence Agency
to support a secret effort to overthrow the Allende government before he
even took office. The effort failed. The United States then moved to cut
Chile off from crucial financial credits, food assistance and spare parts
for machinery, such as trucks and farm equipment, bought in the United
States. The U.S. Ambassador to Chile declared, "Not a nut or bolt will
be allowed to reach Chile under Allende. . . . We shall do all within our
power to condemn Chile and the Chileans to the utmost deprivation and
poverty."[5] Later the Administration secretly channeled more than $8
million through the CIA to support political and media opposition to Allende. After Allende's assassination and the takeover by a hardline military dictatorship, credits and assistance to Chile were promptly
restored. We were seeking detente with the communist superpowers at
the time, but not honoring the electoral process in a tiny democratic
country that dared to choose a socialist government. We clearly pre-
ferred a dictatorship and interfered to help bring it about.

By the early 1980's Central America had become a political caul-
dron. In Nicaragua the Marxist-oriented Sandinist rebels overthrew a
U.S.-backed dictatorship so rife with greed and corruption that much of
the business community in Nicaragua supported the rebels. In Guatemala and El Salvador right-wing governments fended off left-wing in-
surgents through measures that frequently included murders and other
gross violations of human rights. The U.S. government tended to view

all of this in terms of a fight against communism, with relatively little regard for the hunger and oppression that nourished a radical and violent
opposition.

These examples show that the leadership of *both* political parties
has erred in its eagerness to bolster governments that set themselves
against communism, but in doing so it has not led the United States to
pay "a decent respect to the opinions of mankind," which the Declaration of Independence commends to us. Because public opinion also represents great power, this has weakened our influence in the world
community.

Most important of all, our preoccupation with communism has led
to "benign neglect" of hunger and poverty, a neglect which fails mon-
umentally to keep faith with the nation's ideals. Adrift from these moor-
ings, we have lacked the capacity to participate in a global development
program of the magnitude and quality that would once again evoke deep
admiration for the United States. Anchored in our ideals, we could easily ensure a massive, worldwide effort to reduce hunger and poverty.
Providing such leadership entails changes in our approach toward (1)
hunger in our own country; (2) trade; (3) investment; (4) economic assistance; and (5) the military.

8
Hunger USA

In 1967, after nearly three decades of unprecedented economic growth, the nation was stunned by reports of widespread and sometimes extreme forms of hunger in the United States. A team of physicians sent by the Field Foundation documented its findings in various localities throughout the South. Visits by members of Congress and extensive media coverage soon followed. Hunger—extensive and sometimes extreme hunger—had been "discovered" in the world's wealthiest nation.

In the wake of these reports Congress and the Nixon Administration initiated or implemented a number of federal food assistance programs. The most important of these was the food stamp program, which by 1983 was providing food assistance for 22 million people at an annual cost of $12.8 billion. Other initiatives included supplemental food for women, infants and children (WIC) found to be at high nutritional risk; expansion of the school lunch program; and nutrition assistance for the elderly through such programs as meals-on-wheels. The total annual cost to the federal government of these programs in 1983 was $15 billion, but their benefit, even financially, in healthier and more productive citizens far outweighed their cost. For example, a study by the Harvard University School of Public Health showed that every dollar spent on the WIC program saved three dollars in immediate health care costs.

In 1977 the same team of doctors that issued the report a decade earlier returned to the places they had visited and found that severe malnutrition had virtually disappeared, infant mortality had dropped by 33 percent, and hunger-related diseases, along with growth retardation, had decreased by 50 percent. The doctors singled out the food stamp program as primarily responsible for the lengthening and strengthening of lives in those areas, and they called it "the most valuable health dollar spent by the federal government."

Despite exaggerated reports of abuse—actual fraud in the Food Stamp program is extremely low—federal food assistance had brought about impressive gains. Although many of the millions of poor people not participating in assistance programs—and some who were participating—remained nutritionally deficient, the programs had eliminated the worst features of hunger in the United States. Senator Bob Dole, chairman of the Senate Finance Committee and of the Senate's subcommittee on Nutrition, called the food stamp program "the most important social program since social security."

Unfortunately, the 1970's, which produced such dramatic gains against hunger, also brought an economic recession that undermined some of those gains. More people were unemployed and needed assistance, while inflation reduced the dollar value of personal benefits. By the late 1970's pressure had mounted for holding down spending on food assistance. In November 1980 the public voted into office an administration that was committed to massive cuts in domestic welfare programs. A number of developments unfolded. The recession became more severe. Unemployment soared. In 1978 11.4 percent of our population was poor. By 1982, 15 percent was poor. Poverty claimed more than one out of seven U.S. citizens.

The new administration succeeded in getting Congress to make some of the cutbacks it proposed in food assistance programs for 1982 and 1983. These cuts eliminated approximately $2.5 billion in 1983 alone from what it would have cost to keep the program benefits at their 1981 level, thus forcing a reduction in benefits and eliminating many people from the programs. Cuts in domestic assistance programs for poor people further eroded their food purchasing power. At the same time the administration proposed, and Congress enacted, huge tax cuts that produced a windfall for people in the highest income brackets. The tax cuts primarily helped the rich, while the program cuts hurt the poor. According to the projections by the Congressional Budget Office, the cuts of 1981 and 1982 promised, from 1983 to 1985, $55.6 billion in additional income to the one percent of the population with incomes over $80,000 a year, while taking $17 billion from the 20 percent of the population with incomes below $10,000 a year.

By the early 1980's hunger, which had dramatically declined during the 1970's, was once more on the rise, despite mounting food surpluses on U.S. farms. The 1983 U.S. Conference of Mayors reported that "hunger is probably the most prevalent and the most insidious" problem facing our cities. In urban centers across the nation, food pantries and soup kitchens sprang up or expanded in response to a sudden upsurge in the number of persons seeking emergency help. The multiplication of hungry people produced the need for more loaves and fishes. By August 1983 President Reagan expressed perplexity over reports of increased hunger and announced the formation of a presidential taskforce to investigate the matter.

Why Are People Hungry?

In the United States as well as in developing countries, people are hungry because they are poor. The greater the poverty, the higher the incidence and severity of hunger.

Being on a food assistance program, even the food stamp program, does not guarantee an adequate diet. The food stamp program aims low. It tries to provide a Thrifty Food Plan diet worked out by the U.S. Department of Agriculture. But a family does not get the full amount for the Thrifty Food Plan unless it has no income. In 1983 the average food stamp benefit was 47 cents per meal.

The Thrifty Food Plan provides the basis for determining the poverty line. On the tested assumption that poor people cannot ordinarily afford to spend more than one-third of their income on food, the government arrives at the official poverty line* by multiplying the cost of the Thrifty Food Plan diet by three. Studies have shown that even the least poor of the poor can barely afford this economy diet. A few years ago the Bureau of Budget said of the Thrifty Food Plan's predecessor (an almost identical twin): "The Economy Plan is an emergency diet intended to be used during periods of economic distress. As a permanent

---

*In 1983 the poverty line for an urban family of four was $9,862 a year or $822 a month, an amount 59 percent of the $16,733 that the Department of Labor said was necessary for such a family to maintain a "lower level" standard of living. (The $16,733 figure is based on a Bureau of Labor Statistics figure for 1981 of $15,323 adjusted upward to reflect cost of living increases.)

diet, the Economy Plan fails to provide sufficient caloric value, although minimum levels of other essential nutrients are sustained.'' The Thrifty Food Plan assumes sophisticated planning abilities, refrigeration, transportation and bulk purchases—advantages that some families lack. In effect, the food stamp program alleviates, but does not always eliminate hunger for those who participate.

However, millions of poor people do not participate in the food stamp program. In 1983 there were 34.4 million poor people in the United States, but only 22 million food stamp participants. Why do so many poor people fail to participate? (1) Pride. Because of the way we treat and talk about people who are on assistance programs, hunger in our country has become the shame of those who go hungry rather than the shame of us who are well fed. (2) Complications. Sometimes people don't know they are eligible for assistance. Enrollment often involves traveling long distances several times, waiting for hours, answering personal questions and providing documented proof of eligibility. (3) County centers are often understaffed and sometimes, rather than seeking out eligible persons, do what they can to discourage applications.

These factors help to explain why many of our country's people are hungry. But behind these factors lurk more fundamental flaws: chronic unemployment, wages that keep families of the working poor below the poverty line, incomes too low to provide bare necessities for others, and a welfare system that doesn't work well enough. All are problems that contribute heavily to hunger in the United States.

Profiles of Hunger

One of the most alarming trends regarding hunger in the United States has to do with the ''feminization of poverty.'' Two out of three poor adults are women. Between 1969 and 1978 the number of families headed by poor women with minor children increased from 1.8 million to 2.7 million, while the number of poor families with male heads dropped from 3.2 million to 2.6 million. The situation is even more acute for black and hispanic women and children. In 1980, 53 percent of black households headed by women were under the poverty line, 54 percent of hispanic households, and 28 percent of white households. According to the U.S. Civil Rights Commission, "If current trends continue, black and Hispanic female-headed households will dominate the poverty population by the year 2000."

A majority of hungry people in this country probably live in urban areas. For example, Anna Hurst is a single mother who works full-time as a typist, earning $141.50 a week. After paying rent, transportation and other fixed monthly costs, Mrs. Hurst has $46 per week in cash and $16 in food stamps to buy food, household supplies and clothes and to cover all other expenses. Some nights the Hursts eat only potatoes for dinner. Some evenings they eat rice with margarine, other nights canned beans. Some nights they have only cold cereal.

The Hurst family was among 9,600 recipients of Aid to Families with Dependent Children (AFDC) and 16,000 food stamp recipients in New York City whose benefits were severely cut or eliminated in 1982. Virtually all were working people. With almost no food in the house and little money to buy any, Mrs. Hurst is often frantic. "It makes you want to say, 'I'll quit my job and stay home and get welfare,' " she told *The New York Times*. "The only thing I won't get that way is respect, because people think if you're a welfare recipient, you're the lowest form of dirt."

A little more than a decade ago a nutritional study of six primary schools on Manhattan's Lower East Side, one of New York's most crowded slums, tested 619 children. The diets of almost three-fourths were rated inadequate. One out of six children had a clinical rating of poor, which showed up in such things as excessive leanness and prominent abdomens. Although the relationship between nutrition and educational achievement has not been fully established, there is little doubt that poor nutrition hinders learning. The children in this nutritional study attended schools in which 80 to 90 percent of those enrolled fell below average reading levels. Poor nutrition for them meant a waste of human resources that even in purely economic terms is costly to us.

Many of our hungry people live in rural areas. Billy Joe Long and his wife, Emmy Lou, live with their three-year-old son Bruce in Giles County, Tennessee. Mr. Long formerly worked as a sharecropper, but by early 1984 had been unemployed for two years. The Longs draw no welfare income because Tennessee is one of 27 states that does not cover needy families with children in which there are two able-bodied parents present in the home. Mr. Long tries to get odd jobs. "I'll do anything I can for people to make a few dollars," he says. Some months he makes $40, but he has made as little as $10. The family lives in a tiny, dilapidated trailer on land owned by Mrs. Long's cousin, so they pay no rent. They rely heavily on donated clothing. Their primary source of income is $184 a month that the family gets in food stamps—the full allotment. They purchase a month's supply of flour, cereal, beans and potatoes and the rest they buy as they are able. But they are driven to sell or exchange some of their food in order to obtain essentials such as soap, electricity, transportation, clothes and drugstore items. The food does not always last for a month. "I've set back many times and let my wife and child eat first. Then, if there was any left, I ate what was left," says Billy Joe Long.

The Longs, like so many other U.S. families, are only marginally short of food. Their level of hunger is one that millions of others around the world aspire to. Nevertheless it occurs in our land of plenty.

The Longs illustrate the fact that most hungry persons in this country are white, although hunger claims a far higher percentage of nonwhites. The Long family also reminds us that hunger and poverty are disproportionately concentrated among rural people, especially in the South and in Appalachia.

Many of the rural hungry are migrant farm workers, a group that the late Edward R. Murrow described in a 1960 CBS documentary, "Harvest of Shame." On that broadcast one of the farmers said, "We used to own our slaves. Now we just rent 'em." Ten years later an NBC documentary, "Migrant," showed that slaves were still being rented. In 1981 migrant workers averaged an annual income, including non-farm earnings, of $3,995, a figure that does not include illegal aliens doing migrant farm work. Migrant workers rank among the worst housed, least educated and least protected by law, with neither health insurance nor unemployment insurance, usually no vote—and often no food assistance.

Among segments of the U.S. population that experience hunger disproportionately, federal statistics point especially to native Americans (Indians). They have the lowest per capita income of any U.S. population group. They suffer the most malnutrition, the most illness, the highest infant mortality rate and the lowest life expectancy of any group

in the United States. This tragic situation has to be one of the bitter iron-
ies of the nation's history.

Steps to End Hunger

The fact that the richest nation on earth has within its borders a sizable population of poor and hungry people does no particular honor to
us. Not another wealthy, industrialized nation, East or West, tolerates
the kind of slums, the persistent unemployment, the lack of medical coverage, or the hunger that still characterizes the United States. Japan, for
example, wiped out hunger years ago. All Japanese school children are
furnished scientifically balanced lunches with nutrients added. Pregnant
mothers and young children get special attention, with a food supple-
ment program available to all mothers during and after pregnancy. The
WIC program in this country serves a similar purpose and does it exceedingly well for those who participate, but it is limited to those whose
low incomes put them at high risk; and because of limited funding only
one out of four eligible women and children benefit. Instead of being relief-oriented, Japan's feeding programs are considered a fundamental investment in the nation.

Even China, despite its great poverty and a population of more than
one billion people, has largely eliminated hunger.

Compared to many other accomplishments, it would be a relatively
easy matter to end hunger in this country.

1. *We could establish a national nutrition policy that assures every
citizen an adequate diet.* Such a policy would go a long way toward res-
cuing the idea of good nutrition from the stigma of welfarism and putting
it on a positive basis. It would be consistent with the right-to-food resolutions passed by Congress in 1976 and the Universal Declaration of
Human Rights.

2. *We could establish a system for monitoring nutrition.* We don't
know how many hungry people there are in the United States. We gather
intricate data about distant planets and galaxies at enormous cost, but we
can only make rough guesses about the extent, severity and causes of
hunger. A nutritional monitoring system is needed to provide basic data
for sensible action. A pilot project along this line was enacted by Congress in 1981 but by 1983 had still not been implemented.

3. *We could improve food assistance.* Japan serves as a useful model, with the food programs mentioned above available to all at no cost, regardless of income. We should offer school lunches, breakfast programs and nutritional help for especially vulnerable persons, such as nursing mothers, infants and the elderly, on the same terms. The food stamp program, too—though properly a stop-gap remedy—could be seen as an opportunity to eradicate hunger and in so doing to safeguard the nation's most precious natural resource: people. But these programs must be adequately funded, as we continue to improve their effectiveness.

4. *We could adopt a policy of guaranteed employment.* If every employable head-of-family had a job that paid a wage by which he or she could sustain the family above the poverty level, millions of poorly nourished citizens would begin to eat well. Such a policy would benefit the entire nation. We have, side by side, jobless people and rotten housing—an unnecessary contradiction; jobless people and children in schools who need more help—a contradiction; jobless people, when parks and recreational facilities need development, streets need cleaning and people need better health services—all contradictions. There are more than enough jobs that need to be done. Why can't we let people do them at a decent wage and increase the quality of life for all of us? Higher technology is eliminating more jobs than it creates. Industrial changes taking place throughout the world are having an increasingly profound impact on the labor force in the United States. These changes and the higher technology that often accompanies them will lead us into more long-term structural unemployment, unless we take innovative steps to prevent this from happening. Can the gains from "high tech" benefit everyone? Or must those gains come at the cost of putting more of our fellow citizens into a social and economic dump?

5. *We could put a floor of economic decency under every citizen.* Guaranteed work would build part of that floor. With guaranteed work in the picture (or without it, for that matter), is it fair to punish children, old people and handicapped people—those who cannot or should not work—by forcing them to live in poverty? They also need an income that lifts them above this level. That could be done through a negative income tax or a guaranteed income similar to social security. Establishing this floor of economic decency would allow us to phase out the food stamp program and the present inadequate welfare system.

Why, with our wealth, has widespread hunger been permitted to exist in the United States? Part of the answer lies in a long history of devotion to a particular understanding of free enterprise that exalts financial success, while branding the destitute as moral delinquents. It is a viewpoint that at an earlier period wanted no government restraints on giant monopolies, but at the same time demanded that authorities act to outlaw and forcibly repress the rise of organized labor—all in the name of free enterprise.

The idea that poverty is the result of moral failure has taken a terrible toll in loss of self-esteem among the poor, and in self-righteousness among the non-poor. Both perspectives are so nakedly at odds with the Bible that the currency they have gained even among Christians and Jews is astonishing. Yet people hold this idea with the best of intentions.

People can change, however. Ernest F. Hollings is a concerned Christian who had seen a lot of poverty, but he believed that the poor could climb to prosperity all by themselves if they just tried. "I was a victim of hunger myopia," he admits. "I can't say that I really saw hunger until I went traveling with a Catholic nun, Sister Anthony, in January 1968." Sister Anthony thought Hollings, an active Protestant, meant well and could learn, so she invited him to visit some families in a Charleston, South Carolina slum. On a cold and rainy day they went visiting. According to Hollings:

> Before we had gone a block, I was miserable. . . . I began to understand . . . that hunger was real, and it existed in hundreds of humans in my own home city. I saw what all America needs to see. The hungry are not able-bodied men, sitting around drunk and lazy on welfare. They are children. They are abandoned women, or the crippled, or the aged.[1]

What makes this story a bit different is that Ernest F. Hollings was (and still is) a U.S. Senator from South Carolina. As governor of South Carolina he had refused to admit that the state had a hunger problem. As a U.S. Senator he balked at having a committee of senators investigate hunger in Beaufort County, South Carolina. But after visiting with some of the hungry in Charleston, and later in Beaufort County, Hollings became an ardent supporter of efforts to end hunger in the United States. Senator Hollings concludes his book, *The Case Against Hunger,* with these words: "America, with its great wealth and energy, has the ability to wipe out hunger almost overnight. We can, we just haven't."

Domestic and Global Links

In several ways domestic and global hunger provide sharp contrasts. Hunger in developing countries is far more pervasive and severe than is hunger in the United States. The solutions are not always the same. Five acres of tillable land may offer a golden opportunity to a rural family in Guatemala, but not in Ohio. Another difference is that in developing countries poor people are not, by virtue of being poor, so readily shorn of their sense of dignity. That may be true partly because hunger and poverty there are the lot of so many. They struggle together against the odds and few are apt to regard their own or another's poverty as a moral stigma. In our country, however, poverty stands out in contrast to the affluence of society as a whole. To be poor is often to be marked as a failure and to feel cast out.

At the same time, significant similarities between domestic and global hunger are evident. Hunger anywhere is a result of poverty and is typically accompanied by a condition or feeling of powerlessness. Powerlessness is reflective of inequalities that are built deeply into the social structure, both here and abroad. The nature and intensity of inequalities vary from place to place. In our country, for example, they are partly rooted in a long history of racial discrimination and negative racial feelings. These feelings influence the way we as individuals think about and the way we as a nation relate to hunger issues here and abroad.

Although solutions to hunger are not always identical, the need for self-help opportunities—the chance to make progress through self-reliant development—is the same both here and abroad. This points toward structural reforms as relatively more important than welfare measures. Employment opportunities, for example, are worth more than income assistance, though the latter is needed where the former fails.

Employment also illustrates the complexity of the link between hunger here and abroad. It is not merely that unemployment is a major cause of hunger and poverty everywhere. Unemployment in our country creates enormous pressure for protectionist measures that prevent developing countries from exporting manufactured products to the United

States. These measures, in turn, prevent people abroad from obtaining jobs that might lift them out of hunger and poverty. So unemployment in this country not only increases hunger here. It also impedes progress against hunger elsewhere in an area of critical importance: trade—a topic to which we now turn.

9
Trade: A Hunger Issue

Few people think of trade as a "hunger" issue. However, trade arrangements do more to determine whether millions live or starve than does food and development aid. Sheer dollar comparisons give some indication of this. In 1981 non-oil developing countries earned a total of $321 billion in exports. (The oil exporting countries earned another $272 billion.) By comparison, in 1981 the non-oil developing countries received $35.5 billion in official development assistance—about 11 percent of their export earnings that year. Exports earned $9 for every dollar of aid.

Trade and hunger are linked to economic policies of industrialized countries. People are hungry because they are poor. Many are poor because they have no jobs or are underemployed. Often they lack productive jobs because their country does not have industries that might provide them with jobs. Frequently the industries have not been developed because the products they could turn out would not have access to markets in industrial countries such as our own. And access to the marketplace is limited by trade restrictions because U.S. workers and industries fear the competition. In this way trade illustrates how hunger is connected to U.S. economic policies.

The impact of trade on hunger depends mainly on economic policies within each country. A country may have booming exports; but if export earnings lopsidedly benefit those who are already prosperous, export gains may do more harm than good to poor people. Only if economic policies promote opportunities for the poor and move toward the elimination of hunger, can export growth help to bring about those results.

How Poor Countries Lose Out

So crucial is trade to poor countries that aid, by comparison, has been called a "soft option"—the easy way out. Lester B. Pearson, the late Prime Minister of Canada, once related to a UN official the pressure on a government to prefer that soft option:

You sit at the Cabinet table [he said in effect] and you tell your colleagues that country X, which we have helped before, has asked for another $Y million. The Minister of Finance, to whom you appeal, agrees that he might perhaps be able to oblige with the necessary funds, but the Minister of Trade intervenes and asks whether it would not be more helpful to assist the exports of country X by allowing duty free entry to Z million shirts. There is an immediate protest from the Minister of Labour, who foresees trouble. You hesitate, and, in the end, you settle for the softer option. You give country X another $Y million, not forgetting that it used some of the previous aid funds to establish a shirt factory for the export trade.[1]

Pearson's example illustrates how poor countries get locked into a losing arrangement. The rules for losing include these five steps:

First, start with a period under colonial rule. Most of today's poor countries are left with systems—transportation, communications, cash crops, industries, and others—that were developed to enrich the ruling country. Political independence does not, by itself, prevent those systems from continuing to serve the same purpose.

Second, give raw materials and primary products a low commercial value and let them account for most of the export earnings of all but a few developing countries. With these low-cost materials, companies in the rich nations manufacture high-value products—which account for most of their exports to the developing countries.

Third, let the terms of trade (the relationship of export to import prices) turn against the poor countries. For several decades prices have dropped for the raw materials and primary products they sell, in relation to the manufactured products and advanced technology they have to buy from industrialized nations. In 1982 the International Monetary Fund reported that "Terms of trade of non-oil developing countries have deteriorated to the lowest level in 25 years.'' Graph #6 (p. 112) shows that commodity prices, relative to the prices of manufactured goods imported by developing countries, fell by almost half between 1950 and 1982. Worsening terms of trade mean huge annual losses that constitute a transfer of resources to the rich nations.

Fourth, let many poor countries depend heavily on a single raw material or a single crop. The price for such exports tends to be low and fluctuates greatly. For example, copper accounts for about half of Chile's exports, but in 1982 the market value of copper was only one-third that of 1970. Meanwhile the cost of imports for Chile rose sharply. Or consider coffee. When asked a few years ago what his chances of staying in power were, the president of one Central American country replied, ''It depends on the price of coffee.'' He was a good prophet. The price of coffee fell, and so did the government. The fact that rich countries, as buyers, often exercise a monopoly-type control of prices over many of these products has not helped the situation.

Fifth, slap tariffs and quotas on manufactured goods coming in from poor countries. Rich nations have tended to maintain trade barriers against labor-intensive goods manufactured by developing countries, while reducing barriers on products that they (the rich nations) produce and sell to one another. A break in this pattern occurred in the major international trade negotiations of the 1970's, the Tokyo round, completed in 1979, which benefited all countries, developing countries included. Tariffs on raw materials were reduced by 60 percent, while tariffs on semi- and finished-manufactured products were reduced by 27 percent. The gains on processed and finished products were partly offset, however, by the imposition of non-tariff barriers such as ''voluntary'' agreements to limit exports, as the recession fueled protectionist sentiment.

If poor countries have such handicaps, then the market is not free. It is rigged. Even the lifting of trade restrictions would not make trade fully ''free,'' because countries do not necessarily do business as equals. Rich, powerful countries and companies hold many bargaining advantages. Poor countries do, however, have an abundance of cheap labor. This advantage, along with favorable tax laws and inadequate labor or safety standards, has enabled a few of the newly industrializing poor countries to get some U.S. companies to relocate their industrial plants—many just across the Mexican border. Plant relocations to developing countries have eliminated many jobs in the United States, and the loss of such jobs has understandably nourished support for laws to further protect U.S. industries from foreign competition. On balance, however, trade is an extremely difficult, uphill struggle for most non-oil-exporting poor countries. All of this helps to explain why the *share* of world exports by non-oil developing countries shrank from 24 percent in 1950 to 10.5 percent in 1974, although since then their share has increased slightly.

Poor countries pay, by their own exports, for the vast majority of imports, which are vital to their economic growth. The Pearson Commission in International Development reported that "growth rates of individual developing countries since 1950 correlate better with their export performance than with any other single indicator."[2] This correlation still holds. For those countries no less than our own, exports can mean more self-reliance *if* they are part of a sound development strategy. They can stimulate growth that provides jobs and incomes for people who would otherwise go hungry.

Understandably, poor countries have grown increasingly frustrated by a pattern of trade that seems designed to keep them "hewers of wood and drawers of water" for the rich countries. Out of this frustration poor countries insisted on the establishment of the UN Conference on Trade and Development (UNCTAD) in 1964. This UN agency has repeatedly documented the need for fair trade opportunities, including trade preferences for poor countries and an international monetary system that would do more to support and less to impede development. But their urgings have been brushed aside.

Against this background the oil crisis and a worldwide recession dealt developing countries additional blows. The non-oil developing countries saw their combined annual trade deficits soar from $10 billion in 1972 to $75 billion in 1982. Chronic trade deficits and mounting debts put added pressure on those countries to emphasize exports—a sound strategy in many instances, but difficult to do during a global recession. Moreover an export-oriented strategy can backfire if it leads a country to incur unmanageable debts or to ignore the development of its own markets. For example, crops for export sale may be promoted at the expense of food production for the local population, increasing malnutrition and causing reliance on costly food imports. Or export industries may divert resources from badly needed rural development. In any case the worldwide recession did not exactly provide the developing countries with a seller's market for their exports; yet they were faced with soaring import bills—hardly a combination designed to further their development.

Reducing Trade Barriers

The United States could seek reforms in world trade that would contribute in a major way toward the ending of hunger. To begin with, we could reduce trade barriers. Protective tariffs and non-tariff barriers work a particular hardship on poor countries, which need to develop markets as they industrialize. For us the issue concerns degrees of abundance; for them it concerns human survival.

U.S. tariffs escalate so that they are lowest on raw materials, higher on semi-processed imports, and highest on finished products. The purpose of this is to protect our own labor-intensive industries; but from the standpoint of poor countries, this turns reason inside out. They need, most of all, encouragement to *process* raw materials and to *manufacture* products. Otherwise they are doomed to perpetual subserviance: using their raw materials for the rich nations, who reap most of the profits.

Import quotas work a similar disadvantage. According to one observer:

> Our policy has been to support the industrialization of Latin American countries until it reached the point where some of its products were marketable, and then to jam on the brakes. Thus, the ideal aid recipient, from the U.S. point of view, has been a country which can accept development assistance indefinitely, without making any progress.[3]

In one instance the United States loaned money to a Latin American country for a cotton glove manufacturing plant. After the plant was built, a North Carolina firm placed an order for 12 million pair a year. Upon advice of the U.S. Tariff Commission, however, the White House restricted the glove company to a quota of 20,000 pair, thus jamming on the brakes.

Tariff barriers hand each of *us* a sizable bill, too, in the form of higher prices, along with the inflationary effect of those prices—an annual cost to U.S. consumers of hundreds of dollars per family. In addition, as the World Bank has pointed out, "poorest [U.S.] consumers are worst affected, since developing countries generally specialize in the low-cost goods that take a large part of the spending of the poor." Trade barriers also hurt our export industries. First, by making it hard for poor countries to expand exports, trade barriers sharply curtail their ability to buy from us. Second, they insure that some countries will impose trade restrictions against us or shop elsewhere. Both are penalties of sizable consequences because developing countries have become increasingly important customers. In 1970 they accounted for 29.6% of total U.S. exports. By 1983, with U.S. exports six times higher than in 1970, those countries accounted for 40% of that total—more than exports to Japan and Western Europe combined. In 1982, however—to cite one example—Mexican purchases from the United States plummeted, costing this country an estimated 250,000 jobs, according to administration officials. A lesson from all of this is how dependent we are on one another for economic health. Recession here induces recession there and vice versa. Unless developing countries get on top of their debts and build up their economies—both of which require improved trade opportunities—they will buy fewer U.S. products. And that, in turn, costs our country money and jobs. More important, if trade barriers were reduced, many hungry people would find employment and food.

The issue of jobs is crucial. A high rate of unemployment and production slack in many U.S. industries provoke strong support for measures to protect those industries from foreign competition. But there is almost unanimous agreement among economists that protectionist measures eliminate more jobs than they save. For example, the automotive "domestic content" bill pushed in the early 1980's would, by the estimate of the Congressional Budget Office, cost three jobs for every one saved, and raise the average price of a new car by at least $1,000 and possibly as much as $3,000. While protection to assure *fair* competition may be appropriate in some instances, in general protective measures invite retaliation and can be expected to backfire. More than one out of every six jobs in U.S. industry is dependent upon exports, and approximately 40 percent of our agricultural production is exported. If we impose measures to protect our enterprise, history instructs us all too well that other countries will counter with measures of their own, thus costing us export-related jobs and sales. If countries can't sell to us, they won't buy from us, either. If we advise them to reduce their trade deficits through more exports, while limiting their access to our markets, the real message may be: Don't depend on trade.

U.S. trade deficits prompt a related concern. For many decades U.S. exports exceeded imports. Between 1888 and 1973 we had only two calendar-year trade deficits. Oil prices helped to change that. In 1974 the U.S. trade deficit was $3 billion and began to rise slowly. In 1982 it jumped to $36 billion and a year later the chairman of the President's Council of Economic Advisers said that the trade deficit might reach $100 billion in 1984. The picture is less alarming if our entire balance of payments is considered. The balance of payments includes income from services (in management and technology, for example) and business investments, as well as trade. Though our balance of trade was $36 billion in deficit in 1982, our balance of payments that year was only $3 billion in deficit. In any case, we continued to show a surplus in trade with non-oil developing countries, so those countries have not been the cause of our trade deficits. And economists were saying that the size of U.S. trade deficits would shrink if we brought our federal deficits and interest rates down. Few recommended protectionism.

Protectionism provides a costly solution because in effect it subsidizes our production weaknesses and handicaps our production strengths, a policy that results in *less* real national wealth. "Even minor protectionist measures can hamper the restructuring of industrial economies, postponing the investment in new industries and companies that is needed to revive growth," the World Bank reported in 1983. A great majority of economists stress that in order to maintain a competitive edge, the United States needs to specialize in areas of comparative advantage, such as higher-technology products.

Economist Paul A. Samuelson, winner of the Nobel Prize, speaks for many of his colleagues when he sees the United States (1) shifting its emphasis from manufacturing to services; (2) accepting as normal an unfavorable balance of trade in consumer goods; (3) paying for this through investment earnings abroad; (4) having a more productive economy as a result; and (5) protecting U.S. workers and industries not with trade barriers but with other guarantees—the topic of the last section of this chapter.

Fair Trade

Movement toward free trade is not enough. That still leaves poor countries with terms of trade that have steadily worked against them. A few years ago *The Christian Century* described the squeeze this way:

> Caught between rising prices on their industrial imports and falling export prices—and effectively excluded from exporting their own industrial products—Asian, African and Latin American leaders of all ideological hues have been driven toward a Marxist cynicism about the world economy.[4]

That kind of desperation is hard for us to feel. Nevertheless we get an inkling of it by noting the occasional anger of our own trade officials toward Japan. John K. Jessup summarized the reason for that anger in a 1970 *Life* magazine article, "How the Japanese Got So Rich So Fast":

> . . . the Japanese treat us the way prewar Belgians or the Dutch used to treat their colonies. They buy chiefly our raw materials—lumber, cotton, wheat, coal, soybeans—and sell us a wide range of high-technology, high-profit manufactured goods. If this trend continues, the U.S. trade deficit with Japan could be $4 billion by 1973.[5]

As it turned out, we reached the $4 billion trade deficit with Japan in 1972. By 1983 that deficit exceeded $19 billion. But the point worth noting is that what Jessup described is exactly the position the poor countries find themselves in *vis-à-vis* the United States—only without the resources to make up for it in other ways or the leverage to fight back.

What we need, then, are trade policies consistent with development goals that place the needs of people—poor people in particular—first. In some cases that means placing conditions or restrictions on trade.

Part of the answer lies in *trade preferences* for the poorest countries. In 1976 Congress enacted a General System of Preferences (GSP) that allows certain goods from developing countries to enter our country duty-free. Not all goods are included. The ones that are have a specified limit. And seven of 130 eligible countries account for three-fourths of all

GSP imports—and these seven countries are relatively prosperous. Trade preferences account for only three percent of total U.S. imports. These preferences could be expanded and could focus on poorer countries and poor people within countries.

Congress took another innovative step in trade policy by enacting a *land-for-food* provision in 1983. The provision was part of special legislation that offered trade, investment and aid benefits to countries in the Caribbean Basin. The land-for-food provision seeks to insure that increased production and export of sugar and beef to the United States as a result of these incentives does not remove land from the production of food for local consumption and cause more malnutrition. It also provides safeguards against increased concentration of land ownership. Although the land-for-food provision applies to one small region, it serves as a model that could be applied on a much wider scale for linking trade incentives to basic human needs. In addition to bringing potential direct benefits to hungry people, such legislation sends out an important policy signal, as well, regarding development strategy.

Stability in trade arrangements is also essential. In 1975 Common Market countries signed with 46 former European colonies an agreement to set up a $450 million stabilization fund for 12 basic commodities imported, mostly duty-free, from the 46. This provides them with a type of guarantee roughly similar to government target prices that assure U.S. farmers at least a minimal return on some key farm commodities. It is a beginning, but only a beginning. As graph #6 indicates, the prices of commodities are erratic—much more so than the graph indicates when individual commodities are measured separately.

Stability goes beyond prices and primary commodities, however. Poor countries must know that if they develop a successful industry it will not be put out of business with one stroke of a pen by the President of the United States through an arbitrary shift in tariffs or quotas. Uncertainty about U.S. trade policies often discourages those with wealth in poor countries from investing in domestic enterprises. If you had a million dollars and you lived in a developing country, would you invest it there or put the money in a Swiss or North American bank? Frequently we encourage the wrong answer.

In some cases international agreements on production, as well as prices, could give poor countries a fairer chance. According to historian J. H. Parry, the Virginia colony was saved from economic ruin and al-

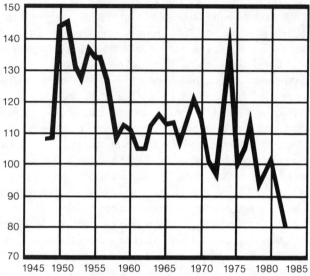

Graph #6: Composite Commodity Price Index, 1948-82

Index, 1977-79 average = 100

The graph shows non-oil commodity prices as measured by the price of manufactures imported by developing countries. The commodities are coffee, cocoa, tea, maize, rice, wheat, sorghum, soybeans, groundnuts, palm oil, coconut oil, copra, groundnut oil, soybean meal, sugar, beef, bananas, oranges, cotton, jute, rubber, tobacco, logs, copper, tin, nickel, bauxite, aluminum, iron ore, manganese ore, lead, zinc, and phosphate rock.

Source: The World Bank: **World Development Report 1983,** pg. 11.

lowed to achieve modest wealth when England agreed to destroy its own tobacco acreage and give the Virginia planters a monopoly on this crop. In the same spirit, adjustments on the part of rich nations today could help to achieve long-range benefits for everyone.

Fair labor standards and the right of labor to organize in developing countries should be encouraged. Such standards could, for example, be made conditions for the granting of trade preferences. Doing so might help to insure that long-term benefits of trade are made available to poor people in those countries. It would also guard against the building of advantages in trade on the repression of poor and working people.

The reforms suggested above would qualify, but not set aside, the principle of free trade. That principle would still apply to trading equals and affect the great majority of exports and imports. By allowing poor countries temporary advantages, however, this approach makes free trade a less absolute goal than fair trade, although it would move the world toward both. By the same token of fairness, countries like our own need to proceed gradually in order to cushion themselves against a sudden influx of products from abroad, and to give their economies time to adjust.

Adjustments at Home

A generous trade policy should be coupled with a thorough adjustment program at home. Labor is rightly concerned about the loss of jobs in industries that face a new competitive challenge from abroad. Workers who face such losses often need assistance for job retraining and relocation—real assistance, not token assistance that amounts to "burial insurance." Business and farm sectors also have serious concerns. Industries that suffer because of foreign imports should readily qualify for low-interest, government-guaranteed loans so that they can become competitive again or move into other areas of production. A U.S. farm program should encourage the family farmer and stimulate world food production, while it discourages competition with developing nations, and that may require adjustments from time to time. The entire nation should share the burden, just as it would share the benefits, of trade reform.

Some of labor's anxiety centers on the exporting of jobs by U.S. firms that transfer their capital and technology to an underdeveloped country, where an affiliate can turn out products at wages that range up to ten times lower than the United States. But if we are to reap the benefits of rationalizing the world's production and distribution, then we must also rationalize production and distribution in the United States so that workers in adversely affected industries can turn to acceptable alternatives.

A key part of the answer is to guarantee employment, in the private sector insofar as possible, but with the government as the employer of last resort. The entire society then assumes the adjustment burden—and the entire society will benefit from a reduction in crime, welfare costs and other problems that plague us partly because of our high unemployment. In addition, we can do more work on long neglected needs, such as rebuilding cities and improving our environment, our schools and our health services.

A companion measure mentioned in the previous chapter would provide a floor of economic decency under each U.S. citizen. A U.S. policy of guaranteed work, together with a guaranteed economic floor for all citizens, is important to the poor countries because its adoption would make possible greater support of a generous trade program. Without such an approach U.S. workers, and those aspiring to work, will constantly fear that gains abroad may eliminate jobs. In this way the nation now generates internal pressure for frustrating the aspirations of hungry people around the globe.

With policies of guaranteed employment and adjustment assistance, various sectors of our economy could play key roles in supporting the extension of trade opportunities that are essential to progress against hunger.

10
The Role of Investment Abroad

Riches convey power. So when a rich man does business with a poor man, the rich man usually has an advantage. Their agreement tends to be weighted in the rich man's favor. If a poor man needs a job, he may (or may not) have to take what he can get on the rich man's terms. As we have seen in the case of trade, dealings between rich and poor persons often have their counterpart in dealings between rich and poor nations. That applies also to investments abroad, which will either assist in the struggle against hunger or do the opposite.

There are two types of investments. Direct investment refers to money or other resources put into a productive enterprise, such as a factory or a farm, in return for a share of the profits. Multinational corporations operating in developing countries represent this type of investment. Loans, the second type of investment, are used for a wide variety of purposes and ordinarily return profits according to a rate of interest agreed upon in advance. This chapter deals with both direct investment and loans.

Like trade, international investment is not seen by the public as a hunger issue, but does much to determine who eats well and who dies. Poor countries depend partly on foreign investments for the capital and technology that growing economies require. Without growing economies their people have little hope of escaping hunger.

To cite one critical example, jobs are at stake. Today in the poor countries unemployment is soaring. People enter the job market not only in unprecedented numbers, but at a *rate* about five times faster than that which today's rich countries usually experienced when they were at comparable stages of development. No wonder, then, that in an *Indicative World Plan* the UN Food and Agriculture Organization calls the problem of employment "far more intractable than that of food supply" in reducing world hunger. Poor countries need investments to generate jobs.

Locating the Issue

If both rich and poor countries are to benefit economically from the comparative advantages of each other, that will happen not only through more enlightened trade policies, but through enlightened investment practices as well. Poor countries need capital and technology; banks and multinational corporations are often effective in achieving that transfer, especially to the newly industrializing (and less poor) developing countries. But can banks and companies invest abroad without building economic empires that do in their own way what the old colonial empires used to do: take advantage of local populations in order to enrich themselves? The question is not one of intent, but result.

The issue is not whether the banks and companies make profits, because without profit-making the transfer of needed capital, technology and skills would not occur. Rather the issue has to do with the size of the profits, control and, most important of all, the impact of investment on the shape of development in any country. Surrounding each of these factors is the massiveness both of developing country indebtedness and of the multinational corporations.

The combined external (foreign) debts of developing countries leaped from $130 billion in 1973 to an estimated $810 billion by the end of 1983, more than 80 percent of it owed to private banks and others at commercial interest rates. During 1983 developing country debts increased by $44 billion. Despite this influx of new loans, developing countries had to pay $21 billion more to the banks than the banks loaned them in 1983, a negative flow that retarded economic growth in many countries.

Various factors contributed to this astounding indebtedness. The oil crisis did so by boosting oil prices from $3 a barrel on the world market in 1973 to $34 a barrel in 1981. As escalating oil prices handed importing countries staggering new costs, the oil exporting countries suddenly had billions of additional dollars to invest abroad. Much of it went to banks in the United States and other industrial countries. The banks in turn needed borrowers for that money. What better way to solve everyone's problem than to recycle the petro-dollars through the banks to the developing countries, enabling them to pay for oil imports?

The blows from successive oil price hikes were compounded by the impact of worldwide inflation and a subsequent recession. The economies of developing countries slowed. The value of their exports declined in relation to the cost of imports from industrial countries. All of this had a devastating effect on most developing countries, which (excluding the oil exporters) saw their combined annual trade deficit jump from $10 billion in 1972 to $75 billion in 1982. These annual deficits drove developing countries to borrow.

To make matters worse, interest rates soared. The fact that high interest rates had roots in U.S. economic policy did not prevent them from adding greatly to the debt burden of those countries.

In retrospect it is clear that, following the 1973 oil crisis, developing countries were driven to borrow out of desperation to pay for oil and other imports in order to keep their economies growing—or simply to keep them afloat. Because a large portion of such loans did not represent new productive investments, many countries eventually could meet their debt payments only by instituting harsh economic measures, and these measures fell most heavily on the poor.

Most of this debt was owed by newly industrializing countries that in the opinion of many economists could, given a turn for the better in the world economy, be expected to meet scheduled payments and reduce their trade deficits. But concern grew that one or more countries in Latin America, where half of the developing country indebtedness was concentrated, might default on their loans and endanger the banking world and the entire global economy. By 1983 some observers had also concluded that Latin American countries could not simultaneously keep up interest payments on their debts, grow economically and avoid social and political upheaval. In any case, 30 of the poorest countries, with a combined population of approximately 300 million and a trade deficit for 1981 alone of $9 billion, were in grave economic difficulty. Most of them, especially in Africa, faced growing indebtedness with stagnating economies and declining per capita food production.

Ironically countries and banks alike felt caught in a debt trap—countries because their payments on those debts were an enormous drain

on their economies, and banks because they risked huge losses or even
bankruptcy in the event of defaults.

If the size of developing country debts prompts concern, so does
the size of multinational corporations and the extent of their global
reach. In 1980 with developing nations and corporations ranked together
on the basis of their total production, 62 of the top hundred were companies, 29 of them (including seven of the top ten) headquartered in the
United States. Exxon's revenues of $110 billion exceeded the GNP of all
but six developing nations: Argentina, Brazil, China, India, Mexico and
Saudi Arabia. Mobil Oil's sales doubled the combined GNP's of Bangladesh and Pakistan, countries with a total population of 182 million.
General Motors' $58 billion compared to a $35 billion GNP for the Philippines. Exxon and General Motors together outproduced India.

The total value of U.S. direct company investments abroad grew
from $32 billion in 1960 to $226 billion in 1981. One-fourth of it ($56
billion) was in developing countries. Since 1970 the United States has
accounted for about half of the new foreign direct investments in developing countries, with a majority of U.S. investments lodged in Latin
America. Although foreign direct investments in developing countries
have grown steadily for several decades, during the 1970's they did so at
a slower rate than GNP growth and domestic investment growth in those
countries. They also declined as a proportion of financial flows (excluding trade) to those countries from 17 to 14 percent. Nevertheless such
flows to developing countries are substantial. They exceeded $14 billion
in 1981.

Company investments in developing countries are not evenly distributed. During 1978–1980 a small group of countries with an annual
per capita GNP of more than $1,000 received 65 percent of these in-
vestments, while low-income developing countries, which included
more than half of the developing country population, received less than
5 percent. In Brazil, an example of the former group, foreign-owned
factories account for 45 percent of the sales of the country's 500 largest
companies.

The size and degree of involvement by multinational corporations
is important because it deeply affects economic development abroad.
Improvements in the way these giant companies do business with developing countries can, therefore, bring enormous benefits to people in

those countries. Corporate size is not in itself negative. The problem—hunger and poverty—is massive, so why shouldn't the answer be big? Small may be beautiful, but it is also small.

The crux of the issue turns on other questions.

The Shape of Development

As in the case of trade, the impact of investment on hunger depends most of all on whether economic, social and political policies within each country generate opportunities for the poor and spread the benefits of development equitably among the entire population or largely bypass the poor. Is a new banana plantation or an auto factory what a poor country needs? The answer depends on who benefits, at what cost, and how that use would compare with alternative uses of the same resources.

Too often countries fail to reach their impoverished citizens with development efforts. Resources may be concentrated on urban industries and neglect agriculture; or promote agriculture for export earnings while neglecting essential food production; or provide a growing middle class with potato chips and barbie dolls, but neglect the poor. Developing countries may borrow heavily from foreign banks to underwrite such development efforts; or they may attract foreign companies by offering generous inducements, such as low-interest loans, over-valued exchange rates or lavish tax concessions.

Sometimes this kind of development is exactly what leaders of poor countries want. But often it happens against their will. They face enormous political pressures and have to choose from limited courses of action. One pressure is that of widespread poverty and unemployment. Other pressures come from those who are not poor but want to improve their standard of living, and from rich people who are determined to become richer. Faced with such pressures, developing country leaders may decide to gamble on an infusion of borrowed money or foreign company investment. If an infusion is part of a sound development strategy, fine. But if, for example, the infusion provides relatively few new jobs for the amount of capital required, country leaders may hope in vain that economic benefits will eventually spread to others or be misguided by the prospect of earning more export dollars.

The Flow of Profits

By the end of 1981 U.S. direct investments in developing countries were valued at $56 billion and yielded a return that year of $12.6 billion, a 22.5 percent rate of return. By comparison the $170 billion of direct investments in industrial countries produced a net income of $19.8 billion, an 11.5 percent return. This indicates a high rate of profit on investments in developing countries, though risks and difficulties often associated with such investments have to be taken into account. Each country needs to determine—in advance, to the extent possible—if the profits that flow out may be excessive and assess carefully whether or not development goals might better be served through other arrangements, such as encouraging new ventures by local corporations.

Often more important than the size of profits are the ways in which those profits are earned. Is a company taking undue advantage of cheap raw materials, cheap labor and various tax havens in order to maximize profits? Are its accounting procedures rigged to send profits to company affiliates in countries with little or no taxation? Is it engaging in price manipulation or bribery?

Loans, too, bring profits. In recent years international loans have outstripped corporate enterprise as a form of investment in developing countries. Principal and interest payments on this indebtedness amounted to $108 billion 1982, compared to $35.5 billion in official development aid to the poor countries. This represents a substantial transfer of resources from poor to rich countries.

One does not need to unearth malicious intent to appreciate the dilemma this poses for developing countries. But it poses a dilemma for our own and other countries, as well. Economic stagnation in developing countries does grave injury to our own economy through lower export earnings and fewer jobs. It is in everyone's interest that those countries be enabled to finance their development without incurring crippling debts.

Control

Both the indebtedness of developing countries and direct productive investments in those countries raise questions regarding control.

No developing country can deal with a massive debt and a sizable annual trade deficit without making extremely painful adjustments. Before blaming countries for getting so deeply into debt, reflect for a moment on the situation they faced: When oil prices soared, they either had to pay more for oil or see their industrial and agricultural output shrink—a far more damaging alternative for most countries. In addition they were encouraged by the industrial nations to borrow in order to recycle petro-dollars so they could keep their economies going and continue to buy industrial country imports. At the same time they were urged to increase their export earnings in order to pay the bills. However, every country, including our own, wants to increase its export earnings and improve its balance of trade, but mathematically all can't do it (my exports are your imports). Because the oil price hikes helped to precipitate and coincided with a combination of problems—growing inflation, a recession, worsening terms of trade and high interest rates—poor countries found themselves in a terrible situation.

The International Monetary Fund (IMF) intervened. The IMF extends billions of dollars of credit each year to countries throughout the world. Globally it has more credit to dispense than any other institution. It can set conditions under which countries obtain IMF financing. That is important in its own right; but more important, private banks follow the lead of the IMF. If the IMF is unwilling to extend credit to a country in financial straits, the banks are also reluctant to do so. As a result, the IMF has enormous control over countries faced with debt problems. The IMF can pretty well dictate (but through negotiation) economic policies that must be adopted if countries are to have further access to credit. That is both good and bad. It is good in that it provides outside pressure for countries to adopt austerity measures when tough measures are needed. It is bad in that the austerity is designed to fall most heavily on working class and poor people. The measures typically require or lead to increased taxes, lower wages, massive layoffs, higher unemployment, less public assistance for food, and cuts in vital services. Such measures would impose severe hardship in any country—in poor countries even more so.

The question of control also applies to multinational corporations. By dominating strategic industries or key sectors of the economy, companies may exercise control far out of proportion to the size of their holdings, which in themselves may be extensive. Even rich countries sometimes protest. In the mid-1960's Europeans began to complain bitterly that U.S. corporations were turning their countries into economic colonies. By consolidating efforts, however, Europe, with its advanced technology and strong economies, stood well against this threat. To a lesser extent so has Canada.

By contrast, consider poor countries with small, weak economies. The impact there is far greater. In 1970 Gunnar Myrdal estimated regarding Latin America that

> . . . directly or indirectly, through joint enterprises and other arrangements, United States corporations now control or decisively influence between 70 and 90 percent of the raw-material resources of Latin America, and probably more than half of its modern manufacturing industry, banking, commerce, and foreign trade, as well as much of its public utilities.[1]

Although U.S. corporate influence and control has declined since 1970, it is still extensive. Globally the trend has been away from direct foreign ownership, though even without ownership foreign companies may still exercise extensive control. For example, multinationals dominate the processing, distribution and especially the marketing of exported farm products. As a result, an estimated 80 percent of the agricultural exports from developing countries remained under the control of multinational corporations in the late 1970's, according to the UN Centre on Transnational Corporations. In this way the influence of foreign companies can be pervasive in low-income developing countries that get much or most of their export earnings from agricultural exports.

Another cause for alarm in Latin America is U.S. dominance in the communications media, which often promote consumer tastes that militate against development needs. You can understand the feeling of people in many poor countries that they are being swallowed up.

Multinational companies may encourage the development of local industries in poor countries—or they can do the opposite. Sometimes local industries sell out to foreign companies. Developing country banks may prefer to lend money to foreign firms rather than to local businessmen or farmers, giving outside companies a big competitive advantage.

Political influence can represent another type of reach for control. The attempt by ITT covertly to prevent Salvador Allende from becoming President of Chile, and later to undermine his administration, is an extreme and fortunately uncommon instance of political intervention. But there are other less dramatic examples of companies seeking improperly to influence government policies in host countries.

Often as important is the effect that U.S.-based companies can have on our own policy toward the countries in which they operate. Because change often shakes stability and creates an atmosphere less conducive to making profits, U.S. business interests tend to discourage our government from favoring needed reforms. This influence helped to scuttle the Alliance for Progress, as investments were talked up and reforms talked down, and has also encouraged the United States to back repressive governments. Hindering civil liberties in this way cultivates for U.S. business a reputation that contradicts the freedom it espouses at home.

This quest by business for stability-without-reform unfortunately dovetails with the State Department's tendency to give stability abroad a higher rating than democracy. Stability is a condition to be greatly desired. But an overriding preference for stability, combined with investment practices that tend to hinder rather than assist the poor, may cause Western industrialists to play into the hands of both communist and right-wing extremists who need above all to convince people that gradualism through democracy offers no hope for improvement.

The Profit Motive

The above concerns raise the question: Are business ventures abroad compatible with the requirements of development in the poor nations? Not necessarily. Private enterprise thrives on the profit motive. Companies go to unfamiliar lands, where the risks and difficulties tend to be abnormal, because they expect to make a return on their investment great enough to offset possible disadvantages. This applies pressure for a "quick kill" on profits, or for excessive long-range returns, a situation that often counteracts healthy growth in those countries. Company representatives may have no idea, or a warped idea, of a country's real development needs and, if so, decisions will reflect this. Evil intent is not a prerequisite.

On the other hand the list of pitfalls does not lead to the conclusion that U.S. business investments are always at loggerheads with the needs of poor countries. Rather it leads us away from the assumption that such ventures *automatically* contribute to healthy development and require no restraints. Many of them do contribute to development; many do not. Just as British capital helped to finance industrial growth in the United States during the last century, so the capital and skills that Western firms now bring to poor countries can be invaluable, *provided they fulfill genuine development needs*. That is a less brash, less arrogant, and perhaps even a less profitable role than the one we are accustomed to. It reflects the real world with painful, stubborn problems, not a tidy, make-believe world whose needs always coincide with our ambitions. But it is a role that can work out to the mutual advantage of both company and underdeveloped country. The model should be that of private enterprise helping to service development for a reasonable return.

Investment Without Empire

As the 1980's unfolded the developing countries faced a difficult future. The oil price hikes that began in October 1973 permanently altered the economic landscape in a way that makes growth far more difficult for most poor countries. A corresponding development that economists feared might also become a permanent part of the world economy was "stagflation"—relatively high rates of inflation along with increased rates of unemployment and slower economic growth, even negative per capita growth in some cases. Few saw an easy or quick way out of the debt trap for developing countries. Indeed, some economists began to speak of it as a debt bomb that might explode and wreck the world economy. Clearly ways need to be found to provide an adequate flow of resources to developing countries without locking them into an impossible situation. Toward this end the basic approach of the World Bank and other international development banks has much to recommend it. They make loans on a project-by-project basis, with each project carefully considered, and charge no interest or very low interest to the poorest nations. One need not approve every aspect of development bank lending to see the advantage of this approach. However, in early 1984 it appeared that there would be little growth in donor countries' contributions to such development banks in the eighties. Yet our economic future and that of others is at stake. More important, the health and survival of countless millions hang in the balance.

For the early 1980's a number of respected economic leaders began calling for an international summit meeting for the purpose of revamping the economic framework to deal with new economic realities. Reforms in the global economy should include, among others, the allocation of additional financial credits to developing countries. In 1970 the IMF began issuing, by simple international agreement, a new form of international credit called Special Drawing Rights. By 1983 $22 billion in SDR's had been allocated, but 70 percent of this went to rich nations and oil exporting countries. The overwhelming need now is for a greater allocation to poor countries. Another reform should be the design of austerity measures that, unlike current IMF measures, would safeguard basic human needs. Austerity may be required for troubled economies, but austerity measures can fall more equitably on the entire society. A third reform would be load-sharing by banks through lower interest rates and stretched-out repayments. A fourth reform might be an international development tax of, say, one percent of each nation's total production; or, failing that, simply a generous increase in untied development aid.

Regarding multinational corporations, more accountability is needed. "The past two decades have witnessed an enormous growth of corporate power at the global level without a corresponding growth of public accountability," wrote Lester R. Brown in *World Without Borders.* That was in the early 1970's when two UN reports, a subcommittee of the U.S. Senate and various books and articles supported the idea of making multinational companies accountable. The issue is complex and controversial, and the possible guidelines for accountability have been evolving slowly. Congress took one step in 1977 when it passed the Foreign Corrupt Practices Act, which prohibits U.S. corporations from bribing foreign officials to win new contracts or influence legislation— previously a tax deductible expense! By 1984 Congress was under pressure to weaken this law.

By 1984 a code of conduct for corporations, developed by the United Nations, had almost been completed with the expectation that it would be considered by the UN General Assembly. It had not yet been determined whether the code would be legally binding or a resolution without force of law, but in all probability it will be a voluntary code.

Either way, primary responsibility for making companies accountable will depend on the development policies of individual governments and conditions they set for the activities of transnational companies.

One option that poor countries have begun to exercise more frequently is that of nationalizing foreign-owned industries. The nationalization of Chile's copper mines is a case in point. Chile has the world's largest reserve of copper. It is of exceptionally high grade, and it has accounted for most of Chile's export earnings. If political consensus is taken as a reflection of popular opinion, then most Chileans—not only socialists—considered the ownership of Chilean copper mines by U.S. companies as a form of outside control no longer acceptable.

Because the U.S. companies had their own processing firms, the government of Chile argued in 1971, they sold copper to themselves at a price well below the world market. The companies made profits alleged by the government—and denied by the companies—to be excessive.

When the Chilean government announced the nationalization of the copper industry, President Allende stressed that Chile was buying the copper industry, not confiscating it. But he insisted that excessive profits be taken into account in determining a fair price. Subsequently the government announced that such profits far exceeded the value of the copper mines and that, therefore, no compensation would be forthcoming. After Allende's overthrow the new military government agreed to compensate the companies. It did not offer to return them, however, because nationalization had been supported by all major parties in Chile before Allende's election.

Nationalization is usually a traumatic remedy. One alternative is to plan at the outset for local ownership, inducing new investments by permitting higher initial profits, but with ownership automatically reverting to nationals after a specified number of years.

In the future it is likely that unrestricted ownership will be increasingly closed to foreigners, and more U.S. firms will export by contract their management and technical skills to the poor countries, sometimes through joint ventures. China, however, announced in 1984 that it would welcome some totally foreign-owned industrial plants and reduce or abolish taxes in order to attract them. Whatever the formulas, it should be possible for multinational firms and poor countries to work out investment agreements that, by serving authentic development needs, contribute to the reduction of hunger.

Both multinational companies and international financial institutions make an enormous impact on developing countries. Whether that impact reduces or increases hunger will depend both on public and private sector decisions regarding the shape of development and the role of foreign investments.

11
Foreign Aid:
A Case for Reform

Foreign aid includes not only food and development aid but also security assistance. In fact by 1984 almost *two-thirds* of U.S. foreign aid was either direct military aid or economic aid given for security reasons. Security aid is treated in the next chapter, where it more appropriately belongs. This chapter focuses on the other third: food and development aid.

Aid for Self-Reliance

"Give a man a fish and you feed him for a day. Teach him how to fish and you feed him for a lifetime."

This oft-repeated Chinese proverb would be easy to ridicule. Look, for example, at the decline in the world's fish-catch and the capital-intensive fishing methods that bring most of that catch to the already well fed rather than to the hungry. Or visit regions where people go hungry and see if they are near water swarming with fish, lacking only someone who can show them how to throw in a line. Still, the proverb is useful because it affirms the importance of self-reliance. Assistance should not make people depend permanently on handouts, but enable them to work their own way out of hunger and poverty.

The Role of Assistance

Because the self-help approach to development is crucial, the fact needs emphasis that it is occurring. For example, roughly 99 percent of new investment in poor countries comes from those countries, not from the outside. Furthermore, as we have seen, earned income from trade is nine times the amount of development aid. And, excluding trade, of other outside capital flows that come from industrial countries, approximately three-fourths of them reflect free market operations such as commercial bank loans, workers' remittances and direct investments. Only one-fourth comes in the form of development aid.

Foreign assistance does, however, play an especially important role for the low-income developing countries, which cannot readily attract private capital. For those countries development aid represents approximately 80 percent of outside capital flows (excluding trade), compared to about 20 percent for the middle-income developing countries.

The importance of aid is also evident from the fact that many of today's rapidly growing developing countries, such as South Korea and Taiwan, can attribute much of their economic success to the fact that they received extraordinary outside assistance for many years.

"Money is not the answer," people frequently say. They are right in the sense that successful development requires primarily other inputs, apart from which money won't help much. Each country must use its own resources, chiefly abundant labor. But we cannot escape the fact that even a labor-intensive approach, combined with determined and intelligent effort, requires substantial capital. A simple thing like the use of fertilizer means that poor farmers need access to credit at reasonable rates of interest, and that presupposes a reserve of capital. It may also suggest the desirability of establishing a fertilizer industry, but that, too, has to be financed. When you add the cost of other improvements such as pest control, tools and building materials, the need for money becomes obvious. Determination and muscle are not enough. Furthermore, grassroots leaders should spread throughout the countryside and work with the rural population in teaching a wide variety of skills. The cost of this may be modest in terms of eventual growth, but the cost cannot be wished away.

Food-for-work projects illustrate this further. Under these projects people are paid with food rather than money to do such work as digging irrigation canals or building roads, clinics, schools and storage facilities. Better nourishment is one objective of this program—not surprising when you remember that most hungry people are rural dwellers. Agriculturalist René Dumont says of one area in India that, with extra food

rations to give them needed energy, the workers could have dredged irrigation reservoirs during the off season and prepared rich fields that
would have produced two harvests instead of one each year. Such programs require capital in the form of food and the nonlabor costs of con-
struction. When assistance for them drops, as it did in the early 1970's
when food prices soared, food-for-work projects get cut back. It doesn't
help to say, "Money is not the answer."

In November 1974 the World Food Conference asked that an International Fund for Agricultural Development (IFAD) be established,
with the goal of increasing assistance for rural development from about
$1.5 billion a year to $5 billion annually by 1980. That goal still required that three-fourths of the capital for rural development would
come from the poor countries themselves. But although there was some
progress toward that goal, ten years later—and well past the 1980 dead-
line—the goal was far from accomplished. IFAD had been established,
but despite an impressive record of bringing development opportunities
and higher productivity to very poor farmers, its potential remained
largely untapped for lack of adequate funding.

Through its International Development Association (IDA), a "soft
loan" agency on which the poorest countries depend for much of their
aid, the World Bank has also greatly increased assistance for rural development among impoverished farmers. Although IDA should direct
more of its aid to the absolute poor, the fact remains that it is by far the
single most important source of development funds for the lowest-in-
come nations. But in 1984 the Administration reduced its commitment
to IDA by $195 million a year for a three-year period. The United States
had been asked to increase its pledge by $55 million a year, so the com-
mitment was $250 million short of the request. Because other nations
match the U.S. contribution on roughly a 3-to-1 basis, the U.S. cutback
effectively eliminated $3 billion of $12 billion requested for IDA assistance. A. W. Clausen, World Bank president, said the cut not only con-
demned millions to abject poverty, but also invited political instability.

Outside assistance can provide the difference between hunger and
health, between stagnation and development. The flow of development
assistance is, therefore, a matter of some consequence. That assistance
from 17 Western donor nations (including Japan) has been steadily rising for more than a decade, despite reductions by the United States and
Australia. Total aid dollars are substantial—$28 billion from Western

donors and another $7.5 billion from oil exporting and communist countries in 1982. Nevertheless that amount was dwarfed by the $108 billion that non-oil poor countries were obligated to pay as debt service payments (much of it to commercial banks) that year. This flow of funds from poor to rich nations ignores the reality of world hunger and the benefits that improved development could confer on the entire world.

Targeted Development Aid

Neither aid nor rapid growth guarantees the kind of development that reduces hunger and poverty. During the 1950's and 1960's development efforts centered almost singularly on achieving rapid economic growth. But preoccupation with economic growth rested on two faulty assumptions. One widely held assumption was that growth should occur primarily in industry. A second assumption was that the benefits of growth would automatically trickle down to poor people. Some benefits did trickle down, but not enough. One of the major lessons from those two decades was, in the words of a World Bank report, "a growing worldwide recognition that economic growth was not reaching the poor majority in many developing societies."[1] As a result, in the early 1970's most national and international development agencies began to place more emphasis on direct measures to alleviate poverty, especially, but not only, in rural areas. In the United States, Congress enacted a mandate for "New Directions" in its foreign aid legislation of 1973 in order to refocus aid toward the meeting of basic human needs among the poor majority in developing countries.

To state the intent of focusing aid more directly on basic human needs is one thing; to implement that intent is quite another. Although some implementation occurred during the 1970's, the intent was honored more in the abstract than in the concrete. Nevertheless, the evidence from those years showed—and the same World Bank report stated—that emphasis on the alleviation of poverty contributed to rather than detracted from economic growth. However, the need to better implement earlier intentions, along with indications that the Reagan administration might be reverting once again to a "trickle down" approach to aid, prompted public and congressional efforts to enact more sharply "targeted development aid" in 1983. The intent, as before, was to reach very poor people with aid in such a way as to enable them to benefit from self-reliant development.

Why Assistance Has Declined

If the purpose of U.S. aid is to help people out of hunger and poverty, then it falls far short of the mark. One reason for this failure is that *aid to the poor countries, never sufficient to begin with, began dropping in the 1960s.* To say that *insufficient* aid is a cause of failure pays indirect tribute to its accomplishments, without which the world would be much worse today.

Development aid is a relatively new idea. After World War II massive private efforts by U.S. citizens and agencies, together with the help of our government, brought food and clothing to many destitute Europeans. But it soon became apparent that the nations of Europe could not rise quickly from the ashes and rebuild themselves. Spurred by this and by fear of Soviet communism, in 1947 the United States proposed a European Recovery Program (the Marshall Plan). By 1952 the United States had poured into Western Europe $23 billion (about $86 billion in 1983 dollars) in official development assistance, not counting military aid or private assistance. Western Europe seemed well on the way toward a dramatic recovery.

In his 1949 inaugural address, President Truman proposed ''a bold new program for making the benefits of our scientific advances and industrial progress available for the improvement and growth of underdeveloped areas.'' Truman suggested that what began for Europe now be extended to the poor nations.

By far the greatest concentration of our aid went to Western Europe. During the four-year period from 1949 to 1952 the United States sent more than $12 billion as outright grants (aside from loans and private help) to Western Europe in the form of official development assistance. By comparison we gave all of Latin America $5 billion in such grants spread over 25 years from 1946 to 1970. During the same 25-year period development grants to all poor countries totalled $40 billion, but $15 billion of that was concentrated in a few countries (Greece, Turkey, Taiwan, Indochina and South Korea) with acute security needs but only 5 percent of the population of all poor countries. To the other 95 percent we allotted roughly $1 billion a year in development grants. On a per capita basis Europe received a concentration of aid several dozen times that of most poor countries.

Why this imbalance? And why has even this assistance tapered off?

For one reason, the people of Europe had millions of close relatives in this country, and countless other U.S. citizens still remembered their European origins. As a result, in virtually every congressional district a powerful grassroots lobby promoted the Marshall Plan. If your member of Congress made speeches about assisting people abroad, he received cheers. He was on the side of the angels and—possibly as important to him—the voters.

In addition, results of our aid to Europe were immediate and dramatic. Countries there already had advanced technology, education, skills and many facilities. They needed a boost to get their disrupted economies going again. But poor countries have none of these advantages. We spread aid to them exceedingly thin by comparison. Not surprisingly, the results disappointed the U.S. public.

Criticism from abroad soured some aid supporters, who felt that recipients were not sufficiently grateful. In recent years the United States and a majority of poor countries have frequently lined up on different sides at the United Nations, and this has corroded support for assistance. "Why should we help them if they oppose us?" people sometimes say.

Aid also tapered off because U.S. taxpayers still think the United States plays the role of Santa Claus in the world. It does not. People have a greatly exaggerated idea of how much this country spends on development assistance. In 1981 the United States ranked 16th among 17 nations that make up the Development Assistance Committee (see graph #7), when aid was measured as a percentage of national production. In 1949, three percent of our Gross National Product went to Europe as assistance. By 1981 U.S. aid to poor countries was $5.8 billion—only *one-fifth of one percent* of our GNP, sharply down even from the early 1960's when it exceeded one-half of one percent of our GNP. While other donor countries combined have been substantially increasing their share of assistance, our contribution has fallen not only as a percentage of national production but also in actual value. Although U.S. aid shows an upward dollar trend, when those dollars are discounted for inflation our aid has declined. For example, measured in constant 1967 dollars, U.S. development aid dropped by one-third, from $3.3 billion in 1961

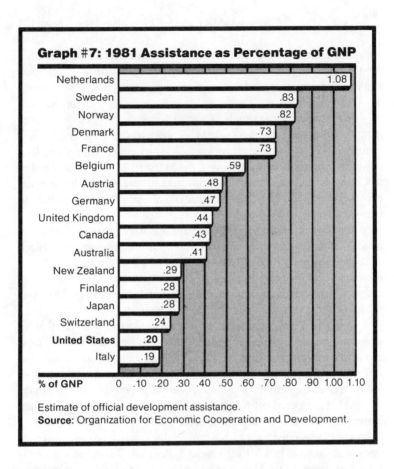

Graph #7: 1981 Assistance as Percentage of GNP

Country	% of GNP
Netherlands	1.08
Sweden	.83
Norway	.82
Denmark	.73
France	.73
Belgium	.59
Austria	.48
Germany	.47
United Kingdom	.44
Canada	.43
Australia	.41
New Zealand	.29
Finland	.28
Japan	.28
Switzerland	.24
United States	**.20**
Italy	.19

% of GNP   0 .10 .20 .30 .40 .50 .60 .70 .80 .90 1.00 1.10

Estimate of official development assistance.
Source: Organization for Economic Cooperation and Development.

to $2.3 billion in 1981. (See graph #8.) In current 1981 dollars it amounted to an average contribution that year of only 7 cents a day per person in the United States.

Neither food nor development aid should be considered an economic loss to the United States. For one thing, nations that are developing become better customers and spur our economy. (In 1982 developing countries purchased $83 billion of U.S. merchandise exports, more than the purchases of Western Europe and Japan combined.) For another, about 70 percent of U.S. bilateral aid and 50 percent of our contributions for multilateral aid (aid given through international devel-

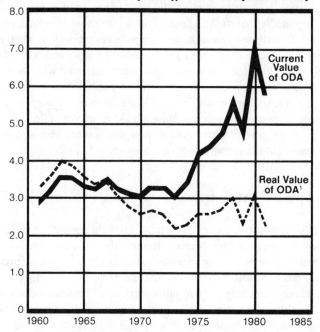

Graph #8: Current Value and Real Value of U.S. Official Development Assistance (ODA), 1961-81 ($ billions)

Current Value of ODA

Real Value of ODA[1]

[1] In constant 1967 dollars.

Note: The "real value" of ODA is calculated by applying a 1967 price index to current ODA values to adjust for inflation.

Source: Overseas Development Council table based on data from the Development Assistance Committee of the Organization for Economic Cooperation and Development, *1973 Review, 1975 Review, 1981 Review,* and *1982 Review.*

opment agencies) are spent on U.S. goods and services, according to a 1983 estimate from the State Department. In addition, in 1982 developing countries sent $1.3 billion to the United States as repayment and interest on previous aid loans. None of this detracts from the fact that aid involves a real contribution of goods and services, as well as dollars; but it does indicate that we get substantial benefits in return.

Despite the embarrassing smallness of our assistance, opinion polls show repeatedly that the U.S. public thinks we should cut back on foreign aid. Surprisingly, though, opinion polls also show the public to be strongly supportive of spending more to reduce hunger and poverty. Evidently the public does not readily associate foreign aid with the reduction of hunger and poverty. That may reflect public awareness that most foreign aid goes for security rather than humanitarian purposes; or a widespread impression that humanitarian aid is not very effective in reducing hunger and poverty. And therein lies another and perhaps the most important reason why U.S. development aid falters.

A Purpose Gone Astray

If U.S. assistance does not adequately help people out of hunger and poverty because it has been too limited, there is another reason why it flounders: *The purpose of spurring development has been sidetracked and aid has been promoted instead for other purposes, chiefly as a tool for stopping communism.* The "other purposes," far from hidden, have been openly used in order to win public support and get appropriations through Congress. Some argue that without these motivations U.S. assistance would have diminished even more. Without leadership, probably so. But in recent years foreign assistance has been increasingly abandoned by humanitarians, within and outside of Congress, who believe that aid has become captive to a mistaken understanding of this nation's role in the world.

What "other purposes" have steered it askew?

Propping up U.S. agriculture played a major part in U.S. food assistance (the Food for Peace Program). Congress enacted Public Law 480 in 1954 to dispose of vast food surpluses. Although the purpose of combating hunger was mentioned in P.L. 480, that law listed a prior objective: "to develop and expand export markets for United States agricultural commodities.'' So cotton and tobacco are also part of the Food for Peace program. P.L. 480 was a great boon to many hungry people abroad, but often it caused more hunger than it cured. Why? Because food aid frequently depressed prices and made it unprofitable for developing country farmers to become more productive. The availability of cheap food also made it easy for policy makers in those countries to postpone their own agricultural development. But when we see surpluses here and hungry people there, it is hard for us to realize that solving our problem—getting rid of our surpluses—might prevent them from solving theirs.

Providing markets for U.S. business has also influenced foreign assistance. Contrary to the impression that recipient nations shop around, almost all U.S. assistance funds used to purchase products are spent in the United States. Bilateral aid is typically tied to such purchases. Periodically, when the foreign aid bill is in trouble, headlines flash, as they did a few years ago in *The Wall Street Journal:* ''U.S. Firms Push to Get Aid Bill Resurrected; The Stakes: About $1 Billion in Annual Sales.''

The main way, however, in which development assistance got sidetracked was for the purpose of combating communism. In part this was deliberate, in part unforeseen. The Marshall Plan followed on the heels of the Truman Doctrine, which declared support for free people resisting internal or external aggression and was aimed immediately at communist threats within Greece and Turkey. So the Cold War played a prominent role even in the European Recovery Program.

Then in 1950, just 20 days after Congress enacted Truman's Point Four Program for aid to poor countries, the Korean War broke out. The impact was stunning. Defense against communism suddenly dominated the entire aid program. We concentrated our assistance in countries where security considerations were uppermost. Until 1970 tiny Taiwan got as much in economic grants as did India. Countries with autocratic and corrupt governments that stood militantly against communism—and often against social reforms as well—were frequently lavished with aid, while neutral countries got comparatively little.

During the Vietnam conflict, and despite famines abroad, Food for Peace became increasingly pressed into the service of war. In 1974 most of our food assistance went to Indochina, where it was sold on the open market to generate money to pay troops and to help faltering war economies.

Or consider the Alliance for Progress. From 1946 until President Kennedy initiated the Alliance in 1961, our development grants to all of Latin America totaled less than $1.2 billion (compared to $1.6 billion for Taiwan during the same period). The Alliance was sold to Congress as a way of preventing Castro from exporting his revolution to other Latin countries. When that danger receded, so did interest in the Alliance. President Kennedy had made clear that success of the Alliance depended on democratic social reforms taking place. Soon after Kennedy's death, President Johnson put Thomas C. Mann in charge of the Alliance. Mann stressed protection of U.S. business investments and neutrality on social reforms. Reforms faded and the Alliance became just another underfunded, unimaginative aid program.

The Rockefeller report in 1969 continued to view structural change in Latin America as a threat against which the United States must strengthen the hand of anti-communist rulers with increased military aid. Consistent with this, the United States withheld aid from Allende's government in Chile, assisted in his overthrow, and promptly restored assistance to the new military dictatorship. In the early 1980's the U.S. response to social and political turbulence in Central America reflected the view that communism, not hunger and poverty, was the underlying problem. That corresponded with sharp successive increases in overall U.S. military and security aid, while development aid continued to decline in real value.

The Alliance had lost its way. But without adequate leadership or a discerning public, so to a large extent had the entire U.S. foreign assistance program.

Aid: Obstacle or Opportunity?

Even if one focuses exclusively on food and development assistance, so much is wrong with our foreign aid program that critics on both the left and the right have urged that it be slashed still further, if not dismantled completely.

Much of the criticism centers on abuse and mismanagement of aid. Some assistance *is* wasted or improperly used. Projects may be misconceived. Food can rot on the docks. Corrupt officials may siphon off aid for personal gain. Inept managers may bungle its administration. Deficiencies in communications, transportation, planning or personnel may cause serious difficulties. Sometimes these problems stem from an insufficient commitment by the donor, not the recipient country. But because these problems are real and not imaginary, aid requires, and usually gets, constant monitoring. The problems are sometimes exaggerated, however, and do not nullify the vital contribution that assistance makes. After both world wars much aid that went from this country to Europe entered the black market; yet those efforts prevented deaths, alleviated suffering and helped people get on their feet. In the late 1970's several million Cambodians were faced with starvation. Emergency aid, quickly arranged by national and international agencies, saved countless lives. The efforts were marred by many mistakes, as well as bureaucratic snarls within Cambodia. But on balance the Cambodian rescue operation must be viewed as a stunning success. Rule of thumb: Do everything possible to prevent abuse and to correct mistakes, but do not throw the baby out with the bath water.

A more serious, if less frequently aired complaint is that aid invariably benefits prosperous people who are in control and who have a stake in maintaining control. By this view, the little aid that does reach poor people is more than offset by larger advantages that it brings to those who already have some wealth and power. They use the benefits of aid to maintain and extend their control over the poor, often leaving them worse off than before. Even as simple a project as constructing a road may increase land values and prompt large landowners to buy out impoverished smallholders, who become landless laborers.

The problem, once again, is real and not imaginary. There are enough examples of aid bringing about precisely this result to fill books; and one can, by compiling such examples, make a strong case against aid. In the end, however, the case does not persuade. Many examples illustrate quite a different outcome—and a majority of efforts fall somewhere in between. The gains cited in chapter 4 regarding dramatically lower infant mortality rates, higher life expectancy and higher literacy levels during the 1960's and 1970's are at least in part attributable to official and private assistance. As with mismanagement and abuse, this case against aid is useful in highlighting deficiencies. But it argues for the improvement of aid rather than its demise.

Reforms

These reforms are needed:

1. *The targeting of more aid to the absolute poor.* A significant move in this direction began in the 1970's, but full implementation has been halting and haphazard. Later, emphasis began to shift from the relative poor—who comprise the vast majority of people in developing countries—to the absolute poor, who include only the poorest third. Success in this area requires more painstaking preparation to make sure that social, cultural and political traditions are taken into account. For example, if projects ignore the role of women in agricultural production, these projects are likely to have an adverse impact on their income. But evidence shows that more careful targeting of aid can bring about growth with equity. We now have experience and momentum to draw on, and therefore an opportunity to greatly improve the quality of our assistance to the benefit of millions of hungry people.

2. *The separation of development aid from military aid.* These two forms of aid need to be divorced, each to be weighed on its own merits. Congress should consider them separately, and the public should not be misled by seeing them lumped together. In addition, security supporting assistance—aid in which military and security concerns are uppermost—should be counted as military aid. Such aid should not be confused with humanitarian assistance in newspaper headlines or in the public mind.

3. *The separation of aid from political considerations.* Complete separation is impossible, but political considerations play much too influential a role and we should eliminate the worst abuses. Emergency food aid, for example, should not be conditioned on whether or not the government of a country facing famine is considered politically friendly. We did well in this respect with Cambodia, less well in the case of Ethiopia. The 1970 report of President Nixon's Task Force on International Development struck the right note when it warned: "This country should not look for gratitude or votes, or any specific short-term foreign policy gains from our participation in international development." But as these lines are written the morning newspaper reports that top State Department officials, including the AID administrator, are supporting a 50 percent cutback in aid to Zimbabwe because that country abstained

on the UN vote deploring the Soviet Union's downing of a South Korean airliner.

4. *A new set of standards on the basis of which assistance can be determined.* These standards should, if possible, be established by international agreement among aid-giving and aid-receiving nations. The standards would include: (a) need; (b) evidence that development is occurring among the masses of poor people; (c) evidence of basic reforms, such as land reform, tax reform, and anticorruption measures, in order to reduce the disparity between rich and poor within a country; (d) efforts to secure human rights; and (e) de-emphasis on military spending. The way a country measured up to these standards would determine how much or how little assistance it could get.

The standards provide a mere sketch. Negotiation and implementation of them would be difficult, but within reach. They could be carried out on a bilateral basis, failing wider agreement; but poor countries might be surprisingly ready to help initiate such an agreement. It would give leaders leverage to do what some of them may want, but fear to do for domestic political reasons.

For example, two decades ago, when Illinois had a serious teacher shortage, some of the state's most highly qualified teachers were unable to get jobs because they were black. The legislature enacted a law saying that before a school could receive state aid, it had to show that it had not discriminated racially in the employment of teachers. Suddenly many school superintendents found it both desirable—and politically acceptable to their school boards—to change employment practices. The motivation may not have been ideal, but the result was good. In a similar way, the carrot of assistance can help countries adopt better development practices.

5. *More careful use of food aid.* Two conditions should govern food assistance. One is an emergency in which famine is present or imminent and the only way to save lives is to get food in fast. The second condition is linking food aid to long-term agricultural development. For example, food-for-work projects can build roads or irrigation facilities; or the proceeds of food sold on the market can be used to supply credit and agricultural extension services to impoverished farmers. Any other use of food aid provides governments with too convenient an opportunity for a ''cheap food'' policy that undermines local farmers, discour-

ages food production, and tends to make countries dependent on food imports when they should become more self-reliant. One type of development-related food aid that deserves attention is its use to help establish an international network of national food reserves. This would give developing countries security to better plan and implement their development.

6. *An increase in development aid, with special emphasis on food production.* The United States could lead the way instead of dragging in support for development aid. In the late 1960's the Pearson Commission on International Development suggested a target of one percent of GNP for donor nations. It was widely accepted as a reasonable goal, then later scaled down by the United Nations to a more cautious 0.7 percent of GNP. By 1982 three countries (Netherlands, Norway and Sweden) had exceeded the one percent target, and two others (Denmark and France) had passed the 0.7 percent target, while the United States lagged far behind.

Can we afford to do it? The question should be: Can we afford not to? A home owner can "save" by not painting his house, not patching his roof, or not fixing a broken furnace. In a similar way we can "save" money by not spending it on urgent world needs, but the real cost of such thrift should be tallied in terms of human suffering and wasted opportunities.

Fourteen days before he died, President Kennedy addressed the Protestant Council of the City of New York and urged church leaders to support foreign aid. He deplored the fact that it had dropped to a mere 4 percent of the national budget (it is less than 1 percent now) and added, "I do not want it said of us what T. S. Eliot said of others some years ago:

'Here were decent godless people;
Their only monument the asphalt road
And a thousand lost golf balls.' ''

Perhaps more to the point, what if the final judgment of history's Lord on Christians in the earth's richest nation is simply, "I was hungry, but you would not feed me"?

12
Let Them Eat Missiles

By an excessive reliance on military power the United States has undermined its capacity to reduce world hunger. As long as the politics of power rather than the politics of justice dominates our thinking, we will do little to assist countries overwhelmed by poverty.

This nation's defense requirements are admittedly enormous and costly. Given the stance of present Soviet leadership, acknowledging the need for reasonable power-balancing, and taking into account the soaring costs of both nuclear and nonnuclear technology, our military spending will be high. But we have exceeded the limits of reason. We depend too much on raw power and pay too little attention to the exercise of power through justice. Various considerations point to this.

The Cost of the Arms Race

The awesome cost of the arms race illustrates an excessive reliance on power.

The United States spent $160 billion for defense in 1981, $187 billion in 1982, and $215 billion in 1983. By 1984 the figure was $231 billion, with projected outlays for 1985 and 1986 of $264 billion and $302 billion respectively. These figures represent a dramatic and unprecedented peacetime military buildup. Consider that:

- U.S. spending for defense exceeds the total annual income of the poorest billion people on earth.
- UNICEF estimates that for every hundred dollars it spends, one child's life is saved. Using this basis, $1 billion on the arms race represents the lives of 10 million children.
- The price of one jet fighter could set up about 40,000 village pharmacies.

- The cost of a tank could provide storage facilities that would, in turn, save enough rice to feed more than 20,000 people for a year. The same money could provide classroom space for 30,000 children.

Worldwide military expenditures reached $650 billion in 1982 and were increasing at the astounding rate of approximately $75 billion a year. *By 1984 world military spending exceeded the total annual income of the poorer half of the world's population.* One half of one percent of that amount would pay for all the farm equipment needed to increase food production to the point of self-sufficiency in food-deficit poor countries. Less than a half-day's spending for arms worldwide would underwrite the entire malaria eradication program of the World Health Organizaton and eliminate a scourge for tens of millions throughout the tropics.

Contrasting military spending with aid given to poor countries, Robert S. McNamara, former president of the World Bank, called it "the mark of an ultimate, and I sometimes fear, incurable folly."[1]

In 1984 the United States devoured approximately $663 million each day in direct military spending—more than the entire annual budgets of the World Health Organization and the UN Development Program combined. The United States allocates about 40 times more for military defense than it does for development assistance. Our annual aid to poor people in Asia, Africa and Latin America is in effect swallowed up every nine days. U.S. officials sometimes excuse our poor record in aid-giving on the basis of our "far heavier share of the common defense burden"—to cite President Nixon's Task Force on International Development. But this rationalizes a let-them-eat-missiles policy.

That policy was vividly illustrated in January 1984. While the Administration was promoting a one-year increase of $47 billion in defense spending, it announced the reduction of this country's annual contribution to the International Development Association by $195 million, to a level that our European allies in a formal message to the State Department called "gravely inadequate." This happened as 22 nations in Africa, which stood to lose the most from this cutback, faced severe drought and famine.

The 1984 U.S. defense budget amounted to an average cost of about $4,100 for a family of four in the United States—a hefty burden—quite apart from interest payments on the national debt (another $1,763), much of which represents postponed payments for defense, or veterans' benefits ($439). The proposed 1984 budget asked every man, woman and child in this country to pay the federal government, on average, approximately:

$1,025 for current military costs
58 for education
58 for housing
42 for natural resources and the environment
23 for development aid to poor countries

At the UN Special Assembly on Raw Materials in April 1974, Secretary of State Henry A. Kissinger said, "The hopes of development will be mocked if resources continue to be consumed by an ever-increasing spiral of armaments." But the mockery continues.

Defense Spending and the Economy

In 1961, shortly after he retired from the presidency, Dwight D. Eisenhower said at the Naval War College:

> . . . We know that the Communists seek to break the economy of the United States—an economy that is based on free enterprise and sound currency. If we, therefore, put one more dollar in a weapons system than we should, we are weakening the defense of the United States.

While more than a sound economy is at stake in military spending, Eisenhower's misgiving was well placed. And today more than in his day, what weakens our economy hurts not only us, but people in developing countries as well.

Military overspend has only one virtue: it creates jobs. But it does so at an exorbitant cost; and, like building pyramids, it constitutes a dead-end use of resources, neither stimulating long-range economic gains nor adding to the quality of life. It results in a substantial increase each year in the amount of the budget that goes for interest rather than for goods and services, thus obligating future federal administrations for immense expenditures over which they have no control.

Put another way, military spending has a negative impact on the following:

1. *Employment.* Although defense spending creates jobs, increasingly that money goes into high technology where the cost per job is also high. The same amount of money can generate more jobs elsewhere.

2. *Federal deficits.* One can argue *how* much, but clearly much of the federal deficit is related to military spending. The 1983 deficit of $207 billion* had a great deal to do not only with a large increase that year in defense spending, but even more with huge defense outlays that over the years built up the federal debt and, along with that debt, interest payments that cost $104 billion in 1983.

3. *Inflation.* Federal deficits spur inflation. So does the fact that production of military hardware tends to be concentrated in a few specialized industries that operate at or near capacity. Additional federal spending in these areas means more competition and higher costs in the private sector for high tech equipment and skilled technicians.

4. *Interest rates.* The federal deficit compels the government to borrow money. The competition for that money drives up interest rates. That hurts us and, as we have seen, each one-point rise in the interest rate on the dollar means an automatic increase of several billion dollars in the annual debt obligations of developing countries.

5. *Economic growth.* Federal borrowing to finance deficits reduces the amount of money available for private investment. High interest rates and low rates of investment slow long-term economic growth. Slow growth in turn means more unemployment, more poverty and more hunger both here and abroad.

In 1983 the Independent Commission on International Development, under the chairmanship of former West German Chancellor Willy Brandt, issued this warning:

> One of the tragic developments of the last three years has been the rise in arms spending. Some think that this will help the world out of recession. In fact military expenditure is very much more a part of the world's economic problem than its solution. At any given level of public expenditure, the higher the

---

*Includes $12 billion in off-budget deficits incurred by the federal government.

proportion of spending devoted to weapons procurement, the smaller the amount of employment created. Military expenditure may also be more inflationary than other public spending. The alleged benefit of technological spin-off is also fallacious; technological advance can be promoted directly with far greater economy.[2]

In addition to all of this is the immediate impact of high defense outlays on poor people. The impact can occur in one or both of two ways: (1) competition for limited funds, and (2) payment for defense. In the early 1980's poor people in the United States clearly lost out in the competition for federal funds, as food and other programs subsidizing their incomes bore an inordinate share of budget cuts. At the same time tax breaks that benefited primarily those in the high income brackets shifted more income to people of wealth and placed proportionately more of the defense spending burden on low and middle income people.

The Military-Industrial Complex

The military-industrial complex has gained too much influence. In his farewell message to Congress, President Eisenhower warned:

In the councils of government we must guard against the acquisition of unwarranted influence, whether sought or unsought, by the military-industrial complex. The potential for the disastrous rise of misplaced power exists and will persist. We must never let the weight of this combination endanger our liberties or democratic processes. We should never take anything for granted.

The new U.S. experience of an immense military establishment has had a "total influence—economic, political, even spiritual," Eisenhower said, and added that it was felt at every level of government. He sensed no diabolical plot, or even, he implied, an evil intention—for the danger exists whether the influence is "sought or unsought." When the military and industrial sectors serve their acknowledged functions, they automatically exercise an enormous power that generates its own momentum. Few others are knowledgeable enough in military affairs to counterbalance their requests. President Nixon's blue-ribbon Defense Panel concluded that not even the President and the Secretary of Defense had staffs competent to evaluate recommendations of the Joint Chiefs of Staff or field commanders.

A military leader, trained to cope with the threat of attack, must plan for the worst possible contingencies. He must suspect an adversary's motives at all times, and is tempted, by nature of his responsibility, to exaggerate the enemy's capabilities. Unless it is carefully controlled, this process may weaken rather than build the nation's security. Robert S. McNamara, Secretary of Defense under Presidents Kennedy and Johnson, has reflected:

> We, for instance, didn't plan to have the numerical advantage that we had in 1966 or 1967 vis-à-vis the Soviets. We didn't need it. The reason we had it was this range of uncertainty that one must guard against, and there's no other way to guard against it than by, in a sense, assuming the worst and acting accordingly. Then, when the worst doesn't happen, you've got more than you need, and that's bad enough. But worse than that is the fact that they see you have it, and they react, and then you've got to do it again. And that's exactly what happened. That's what causes escalation; that is what makes it so dangerous.[3]

McNamara added, "My problem was never to get sufficient money for defense, but, rather, to avoid buying weapons that weren't needed."

In 1960 it was an alleged "missile gap" that triggered more rapid arms escalation in the United States. The gap later proved fictitious, but it figured prominently in the presidential campaign that year. In 1980 it was our "window of vulnerability" to the Soviets that spurred more spending for defense.

If military leaders tend to gather undue influence, so do leaders of industry. Like the military, industry finds itself spilling into a forbidden area simply by doing well what it is expected to do. Anxious to develop and sell its wares to a good customer (the U.S. government), industry pushes the arms race by acting toward the government the way it acts toward any other big customer.

The fact that each contract means jobs and taxes in one or more congressional districts gives defense industries considerable leverage. When the issue of the controversial B-1 bomber first came before Congress, Rockwell International, its chief contractor, argued that even though the bomber was to be built in California, suppliers and major contractors in 48 states would benefit. "If the B-1 were put into full production more than 69,000 persons would be employed directly on the program and an additional 122,700 jobs would be generated or supported" indirectly, said Rockwell.

The government has been a generous customer. In 1970 the General Accounting Office reported that an analysis of 146 defense contracts showed an average pretax profit on total capital investment of 28.3 percent, or roughly twice the normal average for manufacturing profits. Profiteering encourages contractors to invent military improvements and promote their products—which puts them in the business of trying to influence policy.

The effort, technology and money that go into war preparations are matched, astonishingly, by almost no preparation for peace. More than two decades ago Senator Abraham Ribicoff's subcommittee on Executive Reorganization and Governmental Research sent out a questionnaire to 118 major industries, 18 big-city mayors, and seven labor leaders regarding preparations for conversion of industry from wartime to peacetime. Senator Ribicoff summarized the findings this way:

> In general, the responses indicated that private industry is not interested in initiating any major attempts at meeting critical public needs. Most industries have no plans or projects designed to apply their resources to civilian problems. Furthermore, they indicated an unwillingness to initiate such actions without a firm commitment from the Government that their efforts will quickly reap the financial rewards to which they are accustomed. Otherwise, they appear eager to pursue greater defense contracts or stick to commercial products within the private sector.[4]

The situation had not changed by 1983. The government freely plans and subsidizes inflationary war preparations, but is afraid to plan and subsidize peace. By defaulting on that responsibility the government makes itself vulnerable to the unwarranted influence of the military-industrial complex.

Nuclear Overkill

We have long ago passed the point of nuclear overkill. In 1984 the United States had the equivalent of 36 strategic nuclear weapons for every Soviet city of 100,000 or more, while the Soviets had 43 such weapons for every U.S. city of 100,000 or more. The United States had approximately 10,000 strategic nuclear weapons deployed in 1982, and 20,000 tactical nuclear weapons. The Soviet Union had approximately 7,400 strategic and 12,000 tactical nuclear weapons. The Soviets, on the other hand, had the nuclear explosive power perhaps three times that of the United States and more land-based missiles.

The greater Soviet nuclear "throw weight" is, by most analyses, more than offset by the greater accuracy of the smaller U.S. warheads which our military experts prefer. In addition the United States has a more evenly balanced capability that includes submarine-launched missiles and long-range bombers, as well as land-based missiles. These factors, among others, prompted the Presidential Commission on Strategic Forces (the Scowcroft Commission) to conclude in 1983 that U.S. nuclear deterrence was beyond question and not presently weakened by a "window of vulnerability."

The terrifying power that U.S. and Soviet nuclear weapons have can be summed up in a sentence: *It exceeds the destructive force of one million Hiroshima bombs.* If, in a nuclear exchange, only one-tenth of one percent of this power were actually used—an exceedingly optimistic assumption—it would unleash the destructive equivalent of a thousand Hiroshimas.

"Overkill" is the word that has emerged from this nightmare. Each side has the capability of wiping out its opponents many times over, even if one concedes the destruction of most missiles before they are launched as a result of a first strike by the enemy, and adds to that a generous number of failures. The irony is that either side requires only one thing: enough nuclear retaliatory power to discourage the other from striking first. How much would that be? Probably the mere likelihood that several nuclear warheads would reach their target.

How do we account for the impulses that prompt nations to successively higher and more sophisticated levels of overkill? At root may be the instinct that you have to stay (or get) ahead of the enemy because "more powerful means more safe." Any worthwhile steps toward defusing nuclear antagonism involve hidden risks, but not nearly the risk of continuing an arms race that mires both the United States and the Soviet Union more deeply in nuclear terror, increasing their power and paradoxically decreasing the security of each.

Arming Poor Countries

For more than a decade military spending by the developing countries has increased even more rapidly than it has in the rest of the world. In 1971 the developing country share of world military expenditures was 17 percent. By 1980 that share had jumped to 22 percent. That is bad news for hungry people. Money spent on arms is money that poor countries cannot use for desperately needed development. In 1980, 30 developing countries spent more on their military budgets than on health and education combined. More than 30 percent of Pakistan's budget went for defense—$10 for every dollar spent on education in a country with three-fourths of its adult population illiterate.

An increasing proportion of developing country military hardware comes from the superpowers and other countries. Between 1970 and 1980 the total value of arms imported by developing countries grew almost 500 percent, from $3.9 billion to $19.5 billion. Arms exports to Africa, where most countries face declining per capita food production and economic stagnation, increased from $500 million in 1971 to $4.5 billion in 1980.

A study[5] undertaken for the United Nations examined the relationship between defense spending and economic growth in 54 developing countries. In each case higher defense spending was accompanied by slower economic growth—a tragedy for many. The same study found that each dollar spent on arms appeared to reduce agricultural output by 20 cents. In effect these countries were turning plowshares into swords—or jets.

The Soviet Union and the United States (in that order) are the leading suppliers of arms to developing countries, but other countries have also engaged in this lucrative trade that spreads destructive capability around the globe. As Willy Brandt observed, "It is a terrible irony that the most dynamic and rapid transfer of highly sophisticated equipment and technology from rich to poor countries has been in the machinery of death."[6] No longer content to sell only military cast-offs, rich nations are now hawking some of the most advanced weapons.

In 1983 the United States sent $5.4 billion in direct military aid, some as loans, some as grants. Another $2.9 billion went abroad through the Economic Fund, which is military-related aid. (An additional $2 billion in U.S. military exports took the form of private sales.)

U.S. military aid is a hunger issue because it competes with U.S. development aid for funds and because it encourages military spending in countries where such spending inevitably means fewer resources for basic human needs. But it is also a hunger issue in that it tends to reinforce repressive governments that oppose efforts of poor people to improve their lives. In the United States our tradition of liberty is strong enough that the military does not constitute a present danger to freedom. But that is not the case in most nations. Rightly or wrongly, in countries throughout Latin America people blame the United States for some of the worst features of their military dictatorships, because we have trained their officers and supplied them with arms. In 1982 our government announced that it was stepping up military aid to Honduras, the poorest country on the American mainland. The President of Honduras was reported to favor more development aid and felt that the U.S. emphasis on military aid was weakening his government—the first civilian government in a decade—and strengthening the hand of the military. But the military leaders, who had extensive control in Honduras, wanted and got the military aid.

Hunger and Global Security

In relating to developing countries the United States tends to seek military solutions to problems that are primarily social and economic. The problem in El Salvador is not mainly communism, but hunger and extreme poverty, according to Napolean Duarte, the President of El Salvador's ruling junta in 1981. "This is a history of people starving to death, living in misery. For 50 years, the same people had all the power, all the money, all the opportunities. Those who did not have anything tried to take it away from those who had everything. But there were no democratic systems available to them, so they have radicalized themselves, have resorted to violence. And, of course, the second group, the rich, do not want to give up anything so they are fighting.'' But the Administration in Washington saw communism as the main problem, so its main response was to increase military and security aid.

Where a majority of people live in extreme poverty, while those who control the wealth use repressive means to deny opportunity to the poor, you have a society that is ripe for revolution. As people judge their suffering to be neither just nor inevitable, social and political unrest is sure to follow. Such a situation is ripe for communist exploitation—especially if efforts to achieve reforms through moderate means are forcibly crushed.

In 1980 the Brandt Commission said:

> Our survival depends not only on military balance, but on global cooperation to ensure a sustainable biological environment, and sustainable prosperity based on equitably shared resources. Much of the insecurity in the world is connected with the divisions between rich and poor countries—grave injustice and mass starvation causing additional instability.

The same year the Presidential Commission on World Hunger came to a similar conclusion in its report:

> Since the advent of nuclear weapons, most Americans have been conditioned to equate national security with the strength of strategic military force. The Commission considers this prevailing belief to be a simplistic illusion . . . The Commission is firmly convinced that a major worldwide effort to conquer hunger and poverty, far from being a gesture of charity to be offered or withheld according to temporary political whims, holds the key to both global and national security.

A major worldwide effort to conquer hunger and poverty is at least one of the keys to global security. Such an effort, by offering people a peaceful way of improving their lives and the lives of their children, would undermine the appeal of violent revolution. It would be a sound preventive measure far less costly than war.

Overkill and Underfeed

There are various standpoints from which to assess the U.S. military posture. The one that concerns us here is its impact on hungry people. From that standpoint the assessment is this: Excessive reliance on military power has blurred the nation's vision of its founding ideals and diverted us from leading a global effort to end hunger. This is especially apparent in the contrast between soaring military costs and increasingly marginal development assistance. Overkill and underfeed have walked together.

Less than two months after he became President, Dwight D. Eisenhower said, "Every gun that is made, every warship launched, every rocket fired signifies, in the final sense, a theft from those who hunger and are not fed, those who are cold and are not clothed."[7] A more judicious use of power would help to reverse this "theft from those who hunger" by releasing many billions of dollars each year for peaceful development.

Part IV

A Program for Action

13
A Citizens' Movement

In 1968 Barbara Ward, a devout Christian and a well-known development economist from England, took part in an international conference of church leaders and lay professionals. It was a consultation of the Committee on Society, Development and Peace (jointly established by the Pontifical Commission on Justice and Peace and the World Council of Churches) on the question of Christian responsibility in a world of hunger and poverty. Buoyed by the outcome of the consultation, Miss Ward told a handful of U.S. Senators in Washington that the churches in the United States were about to build broad public support for development in the poor countries.

"I'll call you when I get the first letter," responded the junior senator from Minnesota. A few years later Walter Mondale said, "I haven't had to make that call yet."

Why?

Where are the Christians?

Mondale's response underscores a critical "citizenship gap"—failure on the part of the ordinary citizens like readers of this book, who *do* care about hungry people, to express that concern on specific issues to those who decide national policy. Because the decision-makers have not heard from us, they have taken our silence to mean indifference or even hostility to U.S. policies that would help hungry people. As a result, the entire nation has moved increasingly away from the poor countries.

Attempting to change that situation is a young, growing Christian citizens' movement called Bread for the World (802 Rhode Island Ave. N.E., Washington, D.C. 20018). Bread for the World enlists members who in turn contact government leaders on policy matters that have a direct bearing on world hunger. It is a movement that holds promise for helping, with others, to turn this nation around on the hunger issue.

The Formation of a Movement

The idea of Bread for the World began with a handful of Christians in New York reflecting on what the churches were doing—and not doing—about world hunger and poverty. The group concluded that the churches have two great strengths and one critical weakness in this area. The first strength is a solid track record in direct assistance. The church relief and development agencies, such as Catholic Relief Services, Church World Service, and World Vision, have done impressive work. Although Christians could and should multiply support for these agencies, millions do contribute generously to them.

Another strength among the churches has been in official pronouncements. Whether issued by individual leaders, or by agencies or denominations, numerous official statements have been remarkably perceptive about hunger and poverty, and about the need for Christians to respond also in their capacity as citizens.

The problem, in the view of those who spawned Bread for the World, was that these pronouncements were almost uniformly ignored. Christians at the local level were not being mobilized to take action on them. The difference between the *recommendations* of the Sodepax consultation that Barbara Ward attended and the *actual response* that Walter Mondale knew by experience to expect from church members illustrates this.

The churches have the theological basis and fine resolutions, but fail to act on the crucial matter of influencing policy decisions on hunger, the group concluded. And it wanted to change that by organizing, in every congressional district across the land, a nucleus of Christians committed to reaching their members of Congress or other government officials on targeted issues that affect hungry people. They envisioned a "citizens' lobby"—not a lobby of professionals in Washington, but of voters from the grass roots, willing as "folks back home" to advocate the cause of hungry people to their elected representatives.

In the spring of 1973 Bread for the World announced its formation to a small number of people in New York City. Hunger was not in the news. Churches were retrenching on social justice programs. And the organizing committee of seven Protestants and seven Catholics had neither staff nor money. But several hundred persons responded to an appeal for membership at $10 a year—enough encouragement to prompt groundwork for organizing nationally.

By January 1974 Bread for the World had assembled a board of directors that spanned the denominational spectrum: Protestant, Catholic, conservative Evangelical, Episcopal, and (later) Orthodox. Eugene Carson Blake, who had recently retired as general secretary of the World Council of Churches, became the president, and Thomas J. Gumbleton, Catholic Auxiliary Bishop of Detroit, was elected vice-president (later president). And in May 1974 Bread for the World began to recruit members on a nationwide basis.

Ten years later Bread for the World had 45,000 contributing members.

Bread for the World's Vision

Bread for the World aims to attract a broad range of faithful Christians. Most are not political activists, but they are committed to Jesus Christ and share his compassion for others. Many sense deeply their shortcomings regarding world hunger. What they need is a tool that will enable them to work more effectively for long-range remedies. Our citizenship is that tool.

In order to use this tool we need to sharpen our understanding of hunger and its causes. Listening to the poor, keeping an eye on the hunger situation in various parts of the world, watching economic developments, and investigating opportunities for policy change in the nation's capital all play important parts in this process. Bread for the World issues a monthly newsletter that tries to keep its members up to date on these matters. The newsletter features specific choices facing Congress or the Administration that require letters, telegrams, phone calls or visits from members.

Because Christ is the source of our life, Bread for the World considers worship an important part of its basis and program. Local groups are encouraged to plan their activities and discuss issues within the context of reflection on the Gospel, prayer and song. Many worthy church-related projects for human justice have withered on the vine because

Christians did not see the link between their faith and their projects. Bread for the World wants to celebrate that connection.

As the foregoing paragraph indicates, Bread for the World builds not only a network of individual members, but also encourages the formation of local groups. These groups—392 at the beginning of 1984— include area-wide, neighborhood, church and campus units. They give the movement a flesh-and-blood vitality that individual membership alone cannot provide and provide members with mutual support and encouragement. Local groups often spawn leadership for the movement. They offer people an opportunity to work together on projects such as investigating hunger in their own localities. They can reach area churches and multiply contacts with government officials on key issues.

The membership network is organized along state and congressional district lines, so that BFW members can focus on the work of their own U.S. senators and representatives. In this way Bread for the World is able to make an impact at the committee and subcommittee levels in Congress, where legislation is usually won or lost, by getting well-timed messages to senators or representatives who sit on specific committees.

The effectiveness of members in a given congressional district is enhanced by the way districts are organized: with a volunteer coordinator and a coordinating committee at the helm. Most congressional districts have set up "quickline" telephone networks so that when, for example, a crucial vote is suddenly scheduled, public support can be immediately mobilized for a BFW position. In 1984 Bread for the World had 352 "quicklines."

Members themselves do the local organizing. Most local leaders have been prepared through weekend seminars to play an active role. These volunteers come from all walks of life, but some of the most effective are people with no previous expertise on the hunger issue or even any organizing experience, who frequently do a better job of enlisting their peers than do the experts.

Many congregations also relate to Bread for the World as "covenant churches." This relationship involves an intentional commitment on the part of a congregation to deal with the hunger issue on an ongoing basis. Bread for the World, in turn, provides resources for the covenant churches, including a quarterly publication, *Leaven,* which features ideas and activities, as well as worship aids and Bible studies related to the church year.

Members and congregations provide the financial support for more than 90 percent of Bread for the World's work, although grants from church agencies and religious communities have been crucial in getting the movement launched and in supporting new initiatives. None of this money goes directly to assist hungry people—for that donors are referred to their own church agencies. All Bread for the World funds go toward building an effective citizens' movement. Because Bread for the World is engaged in influencing legislation and public policy, funds contributed cannot be deducted from a member's income taxes. (Bread for the World has, however, established a separate BFW Educational Fund which sponsors conferences, does research, produces materials and can receive tax deductible contributions from foundations and individuals.) Salaries at Bread for the World are modest and are based primarily on need rather than on position. In 1984 a staff of 45 was supplemented by the work of 25 interns.

Letters Make a Difference

Can messages from ordinary citizens change decisions in Washington? The answer is an emphatic "Yes!" Don't let anyone tell you that members of Congress pay no attention to their mail. They do—usually through staff members—and they are influenced by what they receive. Rude letters or mimeographed notes may hurt rather than help, of course. But brief, thoughtfully presented points often tip a vote one way or another. Most senators and representatives receive only a handful of letters on most issues and sometimes they receive none. They assume that each letter represents hundreds of other voters who don't bother to write. One letter can make a difference, and a dozen letters will usually make a member of Congress pay special attention. Calls, wires or visits can be even more effective. Examples abound.

1. In 1975 Bread for the World helped draft a Right-to-Food resolution that was introduced in both houses of Congress. Letters of support poured in and in 1976 the House and Senate enacted impressive declarations of intent on hunger, grounded on the right of every person to a nutritionally adequate diet (see Appendix II). Without the letters nothing would have happened.

2. A year later, in the first of many BFW initiatives toward imple-

menting the right to food, Congress enacted a farmer-owned grain reserve. It plays a major role in preventing severe fluctuations in the price and supply of grain, to the benefit of farmers and consumers both here and abroad.

3. In 1980 Congress approved a 4-million ton emergency reserve of wheat for famine relief. Both reserves were narrow victories and neither would have been established except for the letters of support and other contacts from thousands of concerned citizens.

4. In 1979, when millions faced famine in Cambodia, Bread for the World's campaign for a positive U.S. response was well-timed and effective.

5. In 1980 a House committee turned down additional funding for emergency food to Somalia despite a desperate need. However, a last-minute floor amendment, supported by thousands of telegrams and phone calls to members of Congress, substituted $42.8 million in food aid for $100 million in government furniture—aid that proved critical for life and health. Similar aid was later obtained for famine in Ethiopia.

6. In 1983 a Preventing Hunger at Home resolution served as a rallying point in Congress for fending off cuts in domestic food programs, such as food stamps. Letters to Congress helped prevent further cuts in those programs.

7. A land-for-food provision was included in 1983 legislation offering aid and trade incentives to Caribbean Basin countries. This provision set safeguards against the removing of land from the production of food for local consumption and turning such land into export crop production. A well-conceived proposal, combined with citizen action, brought about the congressional passage of this innovative trade measure.

8. Similar efforts have brought about food and development aid reforms that orient aid toward more self-reliant development and assure that more aid directly benefits those in absolute poverty.

Gains such as those indicated above do not mean that Bread for the World has had only successes. But even when setbacks occur, the expressions of support for measures against hunger from a growing number of voters mean that our leaders are becoming increasingly aware of the relationship between their decisions and the health and survival of others.

Even small efforts can make a big difference. In 1982 UNICEF faced a likely $15 million cutback in U.S. funds. Rapid mobilization of support from BFW members in key states probably accounted for the restoration of those funds. The example is worth noting on two counts. First, UNICEF estimates that, on average, for every hundred dollars it spends a child's life is saved. That means a simple action by a few thousand BFW members resulted in life rather than death for 150,000 children, not to mention improved health for thousands more. Second, it provides a comparison. That same year Halloween collections for UNICEF in this country netted $2.2 million, a worthy accomplishment. How foolish, then, to expend vast efforts to collect $2.2 million for UNICEF and see almost seven times that amount taken from UNICEF by virtue of public indifference to actions by Congress and the Administration.

The above examples are small steps, modest beginnings toward policy changes that would make the ending of hunger a high priority of this nation. That is why more Christians are desperately needed to add their voices of concern to those who decide national policy. Lives are at stake.

The above examples show the futility of making voluntary contributions to world relief, while ignoring public policy decisions. Our neglect of those decisions has wiped out many times over the good effect of our voluntary contributions. The net result is not to alleviate hunger, but to ensure its continual spread.

Does this involve Bread for the World in politics? Not in the sense of advocating one political party above another. Bread for the World always seeks bi-partisan support for its positions. The movement's concern is for people who are shorn of basic human needs, and therefore it is big enough to include a wide range of political viewpoints. However, in the sense of influencing decisions made for the nation by Congress or by the Administration, the answer is "Yes." Without taking responsible part in the political process we turn our backs on hungry people.

Resources of Faith

Most Christians perceive the feeding of hungry people as an inescapable expression of faith, and are conditioned to respond. Not enough, no doubt. But they do give to world relief and help in other ways. These Christians can be further challenged with an appeal along this line: "You want to help hungry people, as God has called us to do? Then acts of charity are not enough. We will lose the battle on hunger if we do not change our public policies. Become a voice for the hungry to your member of Congress."

The urgent need is not for churches *as churches* to enter the political fray (although they must take moral stands), but for *Christians as citizens* to exercise their renewed consciences and contact decision-makers. No one need mistake this response as disregard for the separation of church and state. Unfortunately we tend to confuse the separation of church and state with the separation of religion from life. The latter is pure heresy.

Our citizenship is clearly our most powerful tool against hunger. Jesus' parable of the talents (Matthew 25) has an important application in this regard. We have heard much about the arrogance of power. This parable speaks about the arrogance of powerlessness—or, more accurately, the arrogance of *pretending* to be powerless, when in fact we can use what the Master has entrusted to us to do his work. The nature of that work is not left in doubt, for the parable is immediately followed by our Lord's description of the final judgment, when seated on the throne he says to the gathered nations, "I was hungry and you fed me" (or "did not feed me"). Consequently the parable speaks about the arrogance of pretending to be powerless in the face of hunger. This has been our great failure as U.S. Christians, and it points us to a new sense of responsibility toward the hungry in the exercise of our citizenship for them.

Ironically—in view of Jesus' words in Matthew 25 and elsewhere—it is in their understanding of "last things" that Christians have laid themselves open to the charge of quitting on others, of telling the poor and hungry in effect, "Think about heaven." In the "Peanuts" cartoon rendering of James 2:15–17, Snoopy is shivering in the snow. Two bundled up friends come along, pat him on the head and say, "Be of good cheer!" They walk away, leaving Snoopy shivering in the snow as before, but this time with a question mark over his head. However, the resurrection, far from letting Christians off the hook, gives us the freedom to follow Christ and serve others with hope and fearlessness.

Mark Hatfield, U.S. Senator from Oregon and for nine years a director on Bread for the World's board, put the matter this way to fellow Conservative Baptists:

Precisely because all history is consummated in him—because Christ is Lord over all—we must give our lives in his service to the world's need. In so doing, we are proclaiming and giving witness to his love and victory. We may believe that history will end in utter destruction before the New Jerusalem comes into being. But that should not deter us from ministering to the world's suffering and need any more than the knowledge of the eventual death of every person would lead us to abandon any ministry to sickness and disease.[1]

In an apostolic letter on social justice, Pope Paul VI made much the same point:

Animated by the power of the Spirit of Jesus Christ, the Savior of mankind, and upheld by hope, the Christian involves himself in the building up of the human city, one that is to be peaceful, just and fraternal and acceptable as an offering to God. In fact, "the expectation of a new earth must not weaken but rather stimulate our concern for cultivating this one. . . ."[2]

Many Christians will become citizen advocates for the hungry, if two conditions are met: First, they want to be shown that such a response is crucial for hungry people—an increasingly easy case to make. Second, they must be summoned to such a response by the central events of their faith, chiefly the life, death and resurrection of Jesus. They need to see their baptism as a rising with Christ to a new life in which hungry people have no less place for Christians than they had for Jesus. They need to remember through the feeding of the multitude that to break bread at the Lord's table implies a commitment to enable hungry brothers and sisters to break bread.

Frequently people ask, "The problem of hunger is so complex, so enormous—what reason do we have for hope?" The answer is that Christians do not root their hope in the latest UN projections or some social scientist's analysis of how things may turn out in ten or twenty years. Christians root their hope in God and believe that the future is with his Kingdom, however and whenever it comes. No efforts consistent with this hope are wasted. They are signs of the Kingdom and through them God does his work. The Christian understanding of sinful human nature should spare us from illusions that make so many of today's crusaders tomorrow's cynics. And the Christian hope should give us staying power long after many others have become discouraged or gone on to the next cause.

The Christian orientation of Bread for the World does not give its members a special corner on understanding world hunger. Nor does it deny the deep concern of many others, including Jews, with whom we share the Law and the Prophets. Bread for the World leaves large and important segments of the U.S. public untouched, so there is a clear need for other and more broadly based citizens' movements that include world hunger on their agendas. Bread for the World's special calling is to invite people from within the churches to take their faith seriously, and, as like-minded movements emerge, to work closely with them. Some of these are mentioned in the next chapter.

This appeal to faith is part of political realism. In *The Challenge of World Poverty* Gunnar Myrdal has stressed that idealistic motives can be a powerful incentive for change: "When some of my colleagues believe that they are particularly hard-boiled and scientific in excluding from their analysis the fact that people plead to their consciences, I believe that they are simply unrealistic."[3] Realism suggests that in addressing other Christians we appeal to them on the basis of that which claims our deepest loyalty.

Making a Choice

Each of us helps to decide how our nation should use its power and wealth in a hungry world. If we choose not to get involved, we are helping to make the kind of decisions that lock people into hunger. Put another way, saying nothing to political leaders *is* saying something to them. We usually get the kind of leadership we ask for, and if we ask for none on world hunger, that is what we can expect.

Shortly after the 1974 World Food Conference President Ford commissioned the National Academy of Sciences to undertake a study of world hunger. The NAS was asked to focus primarily on ways in which the United States could contribute to a solution through research and technology. Some 1500 scientists participated in the study, which was published in a 6-volume report in 1977. The report concluded that *lack of political will,* not lack of technology, was the main obstacle. It said, "If there is the political will in this country and abroad . . . it should be possible to overcome the worst aspects of widespread hunger and malnutrition within one generation."

A few years later, in 1980, President Carter's commission on world hunger arrived at a similar conclusion. It said, "Despite the size and the severity of the problem, it is possible to eliminate the worst aspects of hunger and malnutrition by the year 2000—*provided the United States and other countries make this a major policy objective* (italics added)."

These reports highlight two remarkable facts. The first is that the world has the technological capability to end hunger. The second is that we lack the political will to do so. Our challenge, therefore, is to summon the necessary will—to mobilize public support for making the elimination of world hunger a major policy objective of this nation. Because of the pre-eminent position of the United States worldwide, what this country does or fails to do regarding world hunger will set the pace for others. If we drag our feet, other countries will be encouraged to drag theirs. If we take leadership, others will follow.

To a lone individual reading these pages that challenge may seem overwhelming. "What difference can I make?" is our instinctive reaction. But that is the counsel of despair, and despair is unbelief. The evidence shows that individuals *can* make an enormous difference. We can help the nation reach out to a hungry world by adding to our contributions for world relief the offering of our citizenship. Over and over again in Bread for the World's experience, a single letter, one lone meeting with a member of Congress or contact from a small but determined number of voters in one district has garnered a key congressional vote and helped to produce a national decision of vital importance to hungry people.

Your participation in a citizens' movement against hunger is an important step toward ending hunger. The end, however, will not likely be seen in our lifetimes; and no one can even guarantee a less hungry world in 10 or 20 years. That outcome is very much in doubt and to a great extent depends upon what we do or fail to do. Regardless of the trends, however, our efforts will not be wasted. They will mean life and opportunity for others. Furthermore, such efforts, far from diminishing our lives, enable us to fulfill our purpose in life and to celebrate the Kingdom of God more fully.

If we can persuade enough others to take part in this movement with us, we have an excellent opportunity to turn the nation and the world around on the issue of hunger. We can be part of an historically momentous peaceful revolution.

It will not happen overnight.

And it will not be easy.

But it can be done.

The choice is ours.

14
"What Can I Do?"

In the PBS network documentary, "World Hunger—Who Will Survive?", narrator Bill Moyers tells of a friend who, upon learning that the documentary is in process, said, "Bloated bodies! Don't show us any more bloated bodies. I know they are there, but what can I do about it?"

What can I do?

The question is often rhetorical, with the answer implied: "Nothing." Because that expresses the feelings of so many, you may first need to advise yourself that ordinary people *can* do something about hunger. Each person has special abilities that are needed. Not to use them is to bury your talent, as did the servant in the parable. To use them is to offer yourself to God and reach out to others. Though individual efforts may be difficult or impossible to measure, they make a difference. They are like the little ripples that in combination add up to big waves.

Second, don't get discouraged. If you throw yourself into the cause with great enthusiasm but give up when you encounter obstacles or when the newness wears off, you won't help much. But if you can stick to the methodical monotonous tasks that have to be done, you can be a mover. Start small, if necessary, but stick to it.

Third, begin now. If you wait for a better time to come along, it probably won't. So start on some things you can begin to do at once. One step leads to another.

Below are lists of things that individuals and groups can do. The lists are sketchy. You can make your own improvements. The suggestions are not all easy, but they are within reach.

What Individuals Can Do

1. *Become a citizen advocate*. Join Bread for the World (see back page tear-out) and contact your member of Congress on a few key issues. The BFW newsletter will give you specific information.

2. *Give to your church's relief fund or agency*. Overhead is low and delivery of assistance high. These agencies do immeasurable good and deserve greatly increased support.

3. *Become better informed*. Read books, magazine articles, newspapers. Start clipping and develop a file. Learn about (and from) hungry people in your own area. The better informed you are, the more effective you will be.

4. *Interest others*. Share what you learn, but do so winsomely, in a kind spirit, without anger or self-righteousness, always mindful of your own limitations and the humanity of others—including government leaders.

5. *Discuss the problem of hunger in your family*. It needs to be on the supper agenda. Parents especially can do themselves, their children and others a great favor by putting this front and center in family discussions.

6. *Write a letter to the editor on occasion*. Be brief; pick up on a specific issue, preferably one reported or commented on editorially. Mention your member of Congress, if appropriate. He or she is certain to see it.

7. *Reassess your own pattern of life*. Perhaps you can consume less, waste less, eat, drink, drive or air condition less. Cut down or out the use of fertilizer on your lawn. Fast on occasion and use the money saved for hunger relief. Grow a vegetable garden and share the produce with those in need; or set aside for world relief the value of what you eat.

8. *Get your congregation to become a "covenant church."* This is an excellent way of increasing awareness and involving the congregation. Write Bread for the World for more information.

9. *Help to form a local group*. Groups can be formed within churches or across denominational lines or in other ways. If one already exists, take part. Push especially response on public issues.

10. *Help someone in your area*. Find out through your church or social service agency some person or family in need whom you could help. Or help in a local soup kitchen.

11. *Pray.* This belongs first and last. Pray daily for those who do not have enough; for those who lead; for the wisdom to see our own part in the problem; and for grace to take appropriate action.

What Groups Can Do

Most of the items on the previous list apply to groups, and many on this list apply to individuals.

1. *Influence public policy.* Discuss hunger issues. Develop strategy for influencing your member of Congress (or other appropriate leaders) on specific items. Develop a phone network for use when targeted issues arise. Get others in the churches to contact government leaders at the local, state or national level. Arrange a visit with a member of Congress, or invite him or her to a meeting to discuss one or several key issues; but do your homework first. *Always be courteous,* even when you disagree. Do door-to-door canvassing on some key issue to get others involved.

2. *Investigate hunger in your area and take steps to help.* For example, who qualify for food stamps but are not in the program? How can they be helped to enroll? Could a "food pantry" for the hungry be set up through the churches? Groups may already be working on local hunger problems. Find them; learn from them; work with them. Take the initiative where needed.

3. *Worship.* Your group needs spiritual nourishment and support. You may also be able to encourage churches to incorporate elements of the hunger issue occasionally in their Sunday services or liturgies. Have people donate food at each communion service for a community pantry.

4. *Enlist others.* Contact churches in your area; try to get interdenominational participation. If you already have that, move the other way and consider setting up committees in each congregation. Form a speakers' bureau and let churches and other groups know speakers are available.

5. *Have an offering of letters at church.* Get members to write their member of Congress (or the President, etc.) when some key issue arises and place it in the offering basket. Or provide paper, pens and envelopes on tables, with information.

6. *Form working coalitions with other groups for particular goals.*

What groups (local anti-hunger group, grocers, bankers, farmers, labor unions) might be prepared to back specific legislation, if approached? Or take part in some community-wide educational or fund-raising effort on hunger? CWS-CROP might be a useful instrument for the latter.

7. *Sponsor events:* a public forum to find out candidates' views on hunger issues, a hunger dinner, a hunger hike, a food day, a fast day, a car wash, etc. Involve the youth. And senior citizens.

8. *Make resource materials available at church.* Display books, articles, newsletters, photos, announcements of events.

9. *Sponsor a Bible study, discussion series, or a course on hunger.* The church may (or may not) be the place to do it.

NOTE: It is important for a group, as for an individual, to choose carefully. Don't tackle too much. Do only what you can reasonably expect to do well. Keep your major focus clear, preferably on the public policy side of the issue. Expect discouragements, but don't give up.

REACHING WASHINGTON

By mail/telegram/mailgram:

> Congressman/woman _____
> U.S. House of Representatives
> Washington, D.C. 20515

> Senator _____
> U.S. Senate
> Washington, D.C. 20510

> President _____
> The White House
> Washington, D.C. 20500

Mailgrams are $4.95 for 50 words (including address and signature), delivered the next day.

Personal opinion message telegram is $4.25 for 20 words (message only), same day delivery. Call local Western Union office for both.

By phone:

House or Senate members: 202/224-3121
White House: 202/456-1414

Remember the time zones. You can call Washington from Los Angeles, for example, before 8:00 a.m. for 24¢ the first minute, then 18¢ a minute, plus tax.

You can obtain a list of members on key House and Senate committees, as well as a state-by-state roster of the House and Senate, by writing Bread for the World or the Friends Committee on National Legislation.

For detailed information on Congress and federal agencies: *Congressional Staff Directory,* P.O. Box 62, Mount Vernon, VA 22121. $35. *Politics in America,* Congressional Quarterly Inc., 1414 22nd St., N.W., Washington, D.C. 20037. $29.95 for 1984 edition. Each revision, updated to include a new Congress, comes out *12 months after* the Congress begins.

BOOKS

GENERAL WORKS ON WORLD HUNGER AND POVERTY

Agriculture: Toward 2000. Rome: U.N. Food and Agriculture Organization, 1981, 134 pages. No charge. Assessment and projections.

Berg, Alan. *Malnourished People: A Policy View.* Washington: The World Bank, 1981, 108 pages. $5.00. Berg is a leading nutritionist.

Berger, Peter. *Pyramids of Sacrifice.* New York: Doubleday, 1976, 240 pages. $4.95. Development seen by a prominent sociologist.

Brown, Lester R. and associates. *State of the World—1984.* New York: W. W. Norton & Co., Inc., 1984, 252 pages. $15.95. The first of an annual Worldwatch Institute report on how changes in the resource base affect the world economy.

Byron, William J., editor. *The Causes of World Hunger*. Ramsey, N.J.: Paulist Press, 1982, 256 pages. $8.95. Essays by past and present board and staff members of Bread for the World. A 64-page *Study Guide* by Vicki Ross is also available for $2.50 from Bread for the World Educational Fund.

Cahill, Kevin M., editor. *Famine*. Maryknoll, N.Y.: Orbis Books, 1982, 163 pages. $8.95. Essays from various perspectives.

Dumont, René and Bernard Rosier. *The Hungry Future*. New York: Praeger, 1969, 271 pages. $6.95. Still one of the best on agricultural development.

Ensminger, Douglas and Paul Bomani. *Conquest of World Hunger and Poverty*. Iowa State University Press, 1980, 140 pages. $7.50. Reflects decades of perceptive experience in India and Africa.

Gheddo, Piero. *Why is the Third World Poor?* Maryknoll, N.Y.: Orbis Books, 1973, 143 pages. $3.95. Good explanation.

Grant, James P. *The State of the World's Children 1982–83* (and annually). New York: UNICEF, 11 pages. No charge. UNICEF report describes how 40,000 deaths a day could be reduced by half.

Haq, Mahbub ul. *The Poverty Curtain: Choices for the Third World*. New York: Columbia University Press, 1976, 247 pages. $5.95. By a respected economist at the World Bank.

Jegen, Mary Evelyn, editor. *Growth With Equity*. Ramsey, N.J.: Paulist Press, 1979, 241 pages. $4.95. A collection of fine essays.

Knowles, Louis L., editor. *To End Hunger: An Exploration of Alternative Strategies in the Struggle Against World Hunger*. New York: National Council of Churches, 1983, 264 pages. $5.00. A report from a church-university conference.

Lappe, Francis Moore and Joseph Collins. *Food First: Beyond the Myth of Scarcity*. New York: Ballantine Books, 1979, 619 pages. $2.75. Myths about hunger. A critical perspective from the left.

McLaughlin, Martin M. *World Hunger or Food Self-Reliance? A U.S. Policy Approach for the 1980s*. Overseas Development Council Paper 33. Washington: Overseas Development Council, 1982, 50 pages. $3.00. A concise appraisal.

Myrdal, Gunnar. *The Challenge of World Poverty*. New York: Random House, 1971, 518 pages. $2.95. A classic.

Presidential Commission on World Hunger. *Overcoming World Hunger: The Challenge Ahead,* abridged version. Washington: U.S. Government Printing Office, 1980, 29 pages. $3.75.

Sen, Amartya. *Poverty and Famines: An Essay on Entitlement and Deprivation.* Oxford: Clarendon Press, 1981, 257 pages. $11.95. Argues that famines are caused by factors other than food supply.

Streeten, Paul and associates. *First Things First: Meeting Basic Human Needs in Developing Countries.* Oxford University Press, 1981, 206 pages. $8.95. Former World Bank economist on key theme.

Wortman, Sterling and Ralph W. Cummings, Jr. *To Feed This World.* Baltimore: Johns Hopkins University Press, 1978, 440 pages. $8.95. Fine overview with accent on technology.

Hunger in the United States

Amidei, Nancy. *Hunger in the Eighties: A Primer.* Food Research and Action Center, 1983, 130 pages. $10.00.

Hunger in the Land of Plenty, a domestic hunger kit. Washington: Bread for the World Educational Fund, 1984.

Hunger Watch U.S.A. Preliminary Report. Washington: Bread for the World, 1983, 25 pages. $3.00.

Hutchison, Robert. *Hunger in America.* Chicago: Fides/Claretian, 1982, 115 pages. $5.95.

Kotz, Nick. *Hunger in America: The Federal Response.* New York: Field Foundation, 110 East 85th St., NY, NY 10028. First copy free, others 50¢. Report by doctors revisiting in 1977 hunger areas discovered in 1967.

President's Taskforce on Food Assistance. *Summary Report January, 1984.* A view from the Reagan Administration.

Schwartz-Nobel, Loretta. *Starving in the Shadow of Plenty.* New York: G.P. Putnam & Sons, 1981. $12.95.

International Economics

Brandt Commission. *Common Crisis: North-South Cooperation for World Recovery.* Cambridge: MIT Press, 1983, 174 pages. $4.95.

Brandt Commission. *North-South: A Program for Survival*. Cambridge: MIT Press, 1980, 304 pages. $4.95.

Frank, Andre Gunder. *Capitalism and Underdevelopment in Latin America*. London: Penguin Press, 1971. $6.95. An alternative view that underdevelopment of some countries is caused by development of others.

Hansen, Roger D. *Beyond the North-South Stalemate*. New York: McGraw-Hill, 1979, 329 pages. $12.95.

Harrington, Michael. *The Vast Majority: A Journey to the World's Poor*. New York: Simon & Schuster, 1977, 281 pages. $5.95.

Hoogvelt, Angie. *The Third World in Global Development*. Atlantic Highlands, N.J.: Humanities, 1982, 240 pages. $11.00.

Lewis, John P. and Valeriana Kallab, editors. *U.S. Foreign Policy and Third World: Agenda 1983*. Overseas Development Council. New York: Praeger, 293 pages. $9.95.

Renshaw, Geoffrey. *Employment, Trade and North-South Cooperation*. Washington: International Labor Office, 1981, 263 pages. $15.70.

Streeten, Paul. *Trade Strategies for Development: Papers of the Ninth Cambridge Conference on Development Problems*. Cambridge University Overseas Study Committee. London: Macmillan, 1973, 375 pages. 8 pounds. (Distributed in U.S. by Halsted Press, NY.)

Transnational Corporations in World Development. New York: UN Centre on Transnational Corporations, 385 pages. $38.00.

World Development Report 1983 (and annually). Washington: World Bank, 1983, 214 pages. $8.00. (Or a 20-page summary free.)

POPULATION

Brown, Lester R. *Population Policies for a New Economic Era*. Worldwatch Paper 53. Washington: Worldwatch Institute, 1983, 45 pages. $2.00.

Rich, William. *Smaller Families through Social and Economic Progress*. Washington: Overseas Development Council, 1973, 70 pages. $2.00.

Salas, Rafael M. *The State of World Population 1983* (and annually). New York: UN Fund for Population Activities, 8 pages. No charge. Address: 202 E. 42nd St., NY, NY 10017.

World Development Report 1984. Washington: World Bank, 1984. $8.00.

AID

Bolling, Landrum R. with Craig Smith. *Private Foreign Aid: U.S. Philanthropy for Relief and Development.* Washington: The Council on Foundations, 1982, 330 pages. $14.95.

Congressional Presentation by U.S. Agency for International Development (annual). AID Congressional Liaison Office, 320 21st., NW, Washington, DC 20523. No charge.

Elliott, Charles. *Real Aid.* Independent Group on British Aid, 1982, 61 pages. $2.95. Also follow-up report: *Aid Is Not Enough,* 1983. Both are available from McVicker & Higginbotham, Inc., 113 Atlantic Avenue, Brooklyn, NY 11201 at a cost of $2.95 each.

Lappe, Frances Moore, and Joseph Collins. *Aid as Obstacle.* San Francisco: Institute for Food and Development Policy, 1980, 191 pages. $4.95. The case against.

Poats, Rutherford M. *Development Cooperation: 1983 Review.* Washington: Organization for Economic Cooperation and Development, 1983, 250 pages. $24.00.

Sommer, John G. *Beyond Charity: U.S. Voluntary Aid for a Changing Third World.* Washington: Overseas Development Council, 1977, 180 pages. $3.95.

Stevens, Christopher. *Food Aid and the Developing World.* New York: St. Martin's Press, 1979, 224 pages. $30.00.

MILITARY SPENDING

The Boston Study Group. *The Price of Defense.* San Francisco: W. H. Freeman, 1979, 359 pages. $7.95.

Fallows, James. *National Defense.* New York: Random House, 1982, 224 pages. $4.95.

Sivard, Ruth Leger. *World Military and Social Expenditures 1983* (and annually). World Priorities, Inc., Box 25140, Washington, DC 20007. 46 pages. $4.00.

The U.S. Food System

A Time to Choose: Summary Report on the Structure of Agriculture. Washington: U.S. Department of Agriculture, 1981, 164 pages.

Another Revolution in U.S. Farming. Washington: U.S. Department of Agriculture, 1980, 457 pages.

Morgan, Dan. *Merchants of Grain.* London: Penguin, 1979, 519 pages. $5.95.

Prestbo, John A., editor. *This Abundant Land: A Portrait of American Agriculture from the Pages of the Wall Street Journal.* Princeton, N.J.: Dow Jones Books, 1975, 296 pages. $2.95.

To the Church

Byron, William J. *Toward Stewardship: An Interim Ethic of Poverty, Pollution and Power.* Ramsey, N.J.: Paulist Press, 1975, 89 pages. $1.95.

Freudenberger, C. Dean and Paul M. Minus, Jr. *Christian Responsibility in a Hungry World.* Nashville: Abingdon, 1976, 128 pages. $2.50.

Hessel, Dieter, editor. *Beyond Survival: Bread and Justice in Christian Perspective.* New York: Friendship Press, 1977, 222 pages. $4.25.

Mooneyham, W. Stanley. *What Do You Say to a Hungry World?* Waco: Word Books, 1975, 272 pages.

Paul VI, Pope. *Development of the Peoples.* March 26, 1967 encyclical.

Sider, Ronald J., editor. *Cry Justice: The Bible on Hunger and Poverty.* Ramsey, N.J.: Paulist Press, 1980, 220 pages. $2.95.

Sider, Ronald, J. *Rich Christians in an Age of Hunger, A Biblical Study.* Downers Grove, Ill.: InterVarsity Press, 1980, 249 pages. $5.95.

Most church headquarters and publishers have issued books or booklets on hunger and poverty. In addition, the World Council of Churches offers numerous materials relating to development.

PERIODICALS

Among the more important publications are reports and periodicals published by some of the organizations listed not here but in the next section.

Alternatives. P.O. Box 1707, Forest Park, GA 30057. Quarterly newsletter, $6. Alternative Celebrations Catalog, $5.

CARE Briefs. 660 First Avenue, NY, NY 10016. Quarterly on development issues. Contribution requested.

Ceres. A bi-monthly journal of the UN Food and Agriculture Organization. Order from UNIPUB, 205 E. 42nd St., NY, NY 10017. $15/year.

Development Digest. Excerpts, summaries and reprints from books and journals. Published twice a year by U.S. Agency for International Development, $6.75/year. Order with payment from U.S. Government Printing Office, Washington, DC 20402.

Development Forum. Monthly UN publication featuring aspects of development. P.O. Box 5850, Grand Central Station, NY, NY 10017. $10/year.

Foodlines. Monthly newspaper on federal food programs and budget issues. Published by Food Research And Action Center (see listing). $20/year.

Horizons. A monthly magazine of the U.S. Agency for International Development (see U.S. Government listing). Free upon request.

The New Internationalist. 113 Atlantic Avenue, Brooklyn, NY 11201. A monthly magazine on development issues. $22/year.

Nutrition Week. A newsletter of the Community Nutrition Institute (see listing). The most comprehensive coverage of domestic issues. $40/year, then $50 for renewals.

Seeds. 222 East Lake Drive, Decatur, GA 30030. An award-winning monthly on hunger with Southern Baptist roots. $10/year.

World Development Forum. A twice-monthly, 4-page report of facts, trends and opinions in international development. Free upon request from The Hunger Project, 2015 Steiner St., San Francisco, CA 94115.

FILMS AND FILMSTRIPS

Listed below are a few films and filmstrips that serve well as starters for most audiences, plus a list of places for renting (and in some cases buying) audio visuals. You may write for lists or catalogs. Bread for the World Educational Fund has a 2-page list that you may receive if you send a self-addressed and stamped envelope. Do not overlook your *public library,* which may have films on hunger, including some from UNICEF or other UN agencies. *Church relief agencies* (see list of organizations) have films and filmstrips. Your *denominational film library* may be useful. Most films and filmstrips fail to probe public policies much, if at all. Agency films will promote the work of the sponsoring agency.

FILMS YOU CAN START WITH

Everyone, Everywhere, a 15-minute film featuring Mother Teresa's work, $20 rent from Ecufilm.

Remember Me, a 17-minute film by UNICEF and UN Development Program portrays several children around the world. Rent free from Church World Service/CROP.

Rich and Poor: What Can We Do?, a 23-minute film stressing that rich and poor must work together in development efforts in order to overcome hunger. Rent free from Church World Service/CROP.

Outskirts of Hope, a 54-minute film tells six personal stories, shows hunger, unemployment and poverty in the United States in the 1980's. $79 rent for one showing from New Day Films, P.O. Box 315, Franklin Lakes, NJ 07417.

FILMSTRIPS YOU CAN START WITH

The Politics of Hunger, 1984. With cassette. A 13-minute filmstrip by and about Bread for the World, narrated by Steve Allen. $20.00 purchase or $5.00 rent from Bread for the World.

When the Almsgiving Stops, motivational, examines causes of hunger with a focus on Bangladesh, but not issue-oriented. Rent-free from

Mennonite Central Committee or $45 purchase from Bullfrog Films.

Taking Charge: The Struggle for Economic Justice, $15 rent or $60 purchase (and $3 for companion guide) from NARMIC, 1501 Cherry St., Philadelphia, PA 19102, (215) 241-7175.

DISTRIBUTORS

Church World Service/CROP, P.O. Box 968, Elkhart, IN 46514 (219) 264-3102. Has a free-loan audio-visual library on hunger and development issues. Brochure available.

Bullfrog Films, Inc., Oley, PA 19547 (215) 779-8226.

Earthwork, 3410 19th St., San Francisco, CA 94110 (425) 626-1266. Publishes a directory of 300 "Films on Food and the Land," which includes an excellent essay on how to show films, lead discussions, generate publicity, raise money, and avoid mistakes. $1.50 for individuals, $2.50 for organizations and institutions.

Ecufilm, 810 12th Avenue South, Nashville, TN 37203 (800) 251-4091. An ecumenical film/video distribution service.

Maryknoll Film Library, Maryknoll, NY 10545 (914) 941-7590.

Mass Media Ministries, 2116 N. Charles St., Baltimore, MD 21218 (301) 727-3270.

Mennonite Central Committee Audio-Visual Library, 21 South 12th St., Akron, PA 17501 (717) 859-1551, Ext. 233. Has a free-loan audio-visual library with many A-V's on hunger, poverty and development issues. Write for catalog.

New York University Film Library, 26 Washington Place, New York, NY 10003. Specializes in UN films.

Oxfam-America, 115 Broadway, Boston, MA 02116 (617) 482-1211. Has a variety of slideshows and films on Third World development. List of educational resources available.

Public Television Library, 475 L'Enfant Plaza, SW, Washington, DC 20024 (202) 488-5000. Has a large collection of videotapes for sale or rent.

Teleketics, 1229 S. Santee St., Los Angeles, CA 90015 (213) 746-2916.

UNIFILM, 419 Park Avenue South, New York, NY 10016 (212) 686-

9890. Has many films for sale or rent on social, political and Third
World issues. Catalog available.

U.S. Committee for UNICEF, 331 East 38th St., New York, NY 10016
(212) 686-5522. Has many films on UNICEF and Third World development.

University of Michigan Media Resource Center, 416 Fourth St., Ann
Arbor, MI 48109 (313) 764-5360.

World Bank, Audio-Visuals Dept., 1818 H St., NW, Washington, DC
20433 (202) 676-1631. Has films on international development for
free loan. Catalog available.

GROUPS AND AGENCIES

For a more complete listing of organizations, several guides are available:

1. *A Guide to World Hunger Organizations: Who They Are and
What You Need to Know About Them,* by Louis L. Knowles, includes
descriptions and evaluations of about 20 major organizations, primarily
but not only private agencies engaged in direct assistance. Published in
1984 jointly by Alternatives and Seeds and available for $5.00 from Al-
ternatives, P.O. Box 1707, Forest Park, GA 30057.

2. *The Other Side* has descriptions and evaluations of several
dozen groups. Reprinted from the March 1983 issue and available for
$1.50 from 300 West Apsley, Philadelphia, PA 19144.

3. *Who's Involved With Hunger,* edited by Linda Worthington,
lists and describes about 200 groups without evaluation. Published in
1982 for $6.00 (with new edition projected for 1985) by World Hunger
Education Service, 1317 G Street, NW, Washington, DC 20005.

CITIZEN LOBBIES

Bread for the World, 802 Rhode Island Avenue, N.E., Washington,
D.C. 20018. Monthly newsletter and local groups. Membership
$15.

Friends Committee on National Legislation, 245 Second Street, N.E.,

Washington, D.C. 20002. Monthly newsletter. Covers broad
agenda with emphasis on peace issues. Subscription $15.

Impact, 110 Maryland Avenue, N.E., Washington, D.C. 20002. Action
arm of Washington Interreligious Staff Council and Interfaith Action for Economic Justice. Membership $10.50 national, but $20 in
states with Impact affiliates.

Network, 806 Rhode Island Avenue, N.E., Washington, D.C. 20018.
Staffed by Catholic sisters, covers range of issues. Monthly newsletter. Membership $20.

League of Women Voters, 1730 M Street, N.W., Washington, D.C.
20036. Informative materials and local chapters. Membership dues
vary among chapters.

RESEARCH, INFORMATION AND MEMBERSHIP GROUPS

Most church denominations have agencies or task forces on hunger that
offer information. In addition groups that deal with hunger and development issues include:

Association for Public Justice, Box 56348, Washington, D.C. 20011.
Evangelical group, examines Christian role in public realm. Newsletter and reports.

Bread for the World Educational Fund, 802 Rhode Island Avenue,
N.E., Washington, D.C. 20018. Research, publications and conferences.

Center of Concern, 3700 13th Street, N.E., Washington D.C. 20017.
Global justice issues. Primarily Roman Catholic base. Newsletter
and occasional papers.

Church World Service/CROP, P.O. Box 968, Elkhart, IN 46514. Community hunger appeals including walks, fasts, canvasses. Newsletter and AV resources.

Clergy and Laity Concerned, 198 Broadway, New York, NY 10038. Interfaith peace and justice group with local chapters.

Evangelicals for Social Action, P.O. Box 76560, Washington, DC
20013.

The Hunger Project, 2015 Steiner Street, San Francisco, CA 94115.
Formed by EST, promises an end to hunger by the year 2000.
Newspaper four times a year.

Institute for Food and Development Policy, 2588 Mission Street, San Francisco, CA 94110. Research and publications.

International Food Policy Research Institute, 1776 Massachusetts Avenue, N.W., Washington, DC 20036. Research reports and occasional papers.

Interfaith Action for Economic Justice, 100 Maryland Avenue, N.E., Washington, DC 20002. Coalition of religious groups, develops positions, publishes *Hunger* ($18/year) and *Food Policy Notes* ($6).

Overseas Development Council, 1717 Massachusetts Avenue, N.W., Washington, DC 20036. Research and publications. Books and booklets available individually or at $35 a year.

Population Reference Bureau, 1337 Connecticut Avenue, N.W., Washington, DC 20036. Research and publications.

Society for International Development, Palazzo Civilita del Lavoroe EUR, 00144 Rome, Italy. Quarterly publication with membership.

Worldwatch Institute, 1776 Massachusetts Avenue, N.W., Washington, DC 20036. Research, books and monthly Worldwatch papers ($2 each).

World Food Day, 1776 F Street, N.W., Washington, DC 20437. Resource for annual October 16 events.

World Hunger Education Service, 1317 G Street, N.W., Washington, DC 20005. Newsletter $12 and D.C. seminars.

World Hunger Year, 350 Broadway #307, New York, NY 10013. On domestic hunger. Works mainly through the media to educate the public regarding causes and solutions.

DOMESTIC HUNGER GROUPS

The Children's Foundation, 1420 Massachusetts Avenue, N.W., Washington, DC 20005. Analyzes federal food programs.

The Children's Defense Fund, 122 C St. NW, Washington, DC 20001.

The Center for Budget and Policy Priorities, 236 Massachusetts Avenue, N.E., Washington, DC 20002. Reports on U.S. budget and federal social programs.

Community Nutrition Institute, 2001 S Street, N.W., Washington, DC 20009. Publishes *Nutrition Week,* trains local organizers.

Food Research Action Center (FRAC), 1319 F Street, N.W., Washington, DC 20004. Nonprofit law firm and advocacy center. Publishes information guides.

Second Harvest, Fisher Bldg., 343 S. Dearborn St., Suite 516, Chicago, IL 60604. Coordinates national food bank network.

THE UNITED NATIONS

For general information: UN Information Center, 1028 Connecticut Ave., N.W., Washington, D.C. 20006.

For locating documents: Public Inquiries Unit, Office of Public Information, United Nations, New York, N.Y. 10017.

Buy UN publications from: UNIPUB, 205 East 42nd Street, New York, NY 10017.

New York NY 10017 address is also suitable for most UN-related agencies, including:

UN Conference on Trade and Development (information office)
UN Development Program
UN Food and Agriculture Organization (information office)
UNICEF
World Health Organization

U.S. GOVERNMENT

U.S. Agency for International Development, Department of State, Washington, D.C. 20523.

U.S. Department of Agriculture, Washington, D.C. 20250.

Government Printing Office, Washington, D.C. 20402. Allow about six weeks.

PRIVATE RELIEF AND DEVELOPMENT AGENCIES

Each denomination has its own agency or fund for receiving contributions. A few of the major denominational agencies, along with several interdenominational or church-related agencies:

Agricultural Missions, 475 Riverside Drive, New York, N.Y. 10015.
American Friends Service Committee, 160 No. 15th St., Philadelphia, Pa, 19102.
Catholic Relief Services, 1011 First Avenue, New York, N.Y. 10022.
Church World Service, 475 Riverside Drive, New York, N.Y. 10015.
Committee on World Relief (National Association of Evangelicals), 450 Gunderson Drive, Carol Stream, Ill 60187.
Heiffer Project, Inc. P.O. Box 808, Little Rock, Ark. 72203.
Lutheran World Relief, 315 Park Avenue South, New York, N.Y. 10010.
World Vision International, 919 W. Huntington Drive, Monrovia, Calif. 91016.

If you have a community-wide appeal and need an ecumenical approach, *CWS–CROP,* Box 968, Elkhart, Ind. 46514, is a likely vehicle. It works and shares with Protestant and Catholic agencies.

Outside the church you might consider:

CARE, 660 First Avenue, New York, N.Y. 10016.
Oxfam-America, 115 Broadway, Boston, MA 02116.
U.S. Committee for UNICEF, 331 E. 38th St., New York, N.Y. 10016.

SELECTED BIBLICAL REFERENCES

Genesis 1:29-30 (God gives produce to Adam for food)
Exodus 12 (the Passover)
Exodus 16:1-12 (the manna)
Leviticus 19:10-11 (leave a portion of your harvest for the poor)
Numbers 11:4-20 (people greedy for meat)
Deuteronomy 10:14-19 (the Lord secures justice)

Deuteronomy 24:10-22 (render justice)
1 Kings 17:8-15 (Elijah and the widow's flour and oil)
2 Kings 4:42-44 (feeding the multitude)
Psalm 78:17-31 (they did not believe that God could feed them)
Psalm 146:5-8 (the Lord is just, and feeds the hungry)
Proverbs 21:13 (hear the cries of the poor)
Isaiah 3:13-15 ("Why do you grind the face of the poor?")
Isaiah 25:6-8 (the Kingdom as a feast)
Isaiah 55:1-3 (come to table, without praying)
Isaiah 58:1-10 (the fasting that is pleasing to God)
Isaiah 61:1-3 (good news to the poor)
Isaiah 65:11-14 (the Lord feeds his servants)
Lamentations 2:19-20b (your children faint for hunger)
Lamentations 4:9-10 (happier the victims of the sword than the victims
     of hunger)
Ezekiel 34:20-22 (God will judge between the fat and lean sheep)
Amos 5:21-24 (let justice roll down like waters)
Amos 8:4-7 (the wicked exploit their control and power)
Matthew 5:1-10 (the way to live)
Matthew 5:23-24 (first be reconciled, then offer your gift)
Matthew 6:25-33 (verse 33 is the key)
Matthew 14:15-21 (feeding the multitude)
Matthew 15:32-39 (feeding the multitude)
Matthew 25:14-30 (note the context—the passage that follows)
Matthew 25:31-46 (I was hungry and you fed me)
Matthew 26:20, 26-29 (the Lord's Supper; also Mark 14, Luke 22,
     1 Corinthians 11)
Mark 8:1-9 (feeding the multitude)
Luke 3:9-11 (sharing food and clothes)
Luke 4:16-21 (help for the poor and oppressed)
Luke 6:20-21, 24–25 (blessed are you poor . . . you hungry)
Luke 12:13-21 (the rich fool)
Luke 12:32-48 (to whom much is given is much required)
Luke 16:19-31 (the rich man and Lazarus)
Luke 24:30-35 (known in the breaking of bread)
John 6:1-14 (bread for the world)
John 6:25ff. (the Bread of Life)
Acts 2:42-47 (sharing in the early church)

Acts 4:32 (sharing in the early church)
1 Corinthians 10:14-17 (all are one because partake of one loaf)
1 Corinthians 11:17-33 (selfishness in the Christian assembly)
2 Corinthians 8:9-15 (a question of equality)
2 Corinthians 9:6-15 (he gives freely and frees us to give)
1 Timothy 6:6-19 (be rich in generosity)
James 2:14-17, 26 (faith without works is dead)
1 John 3:17-18 (loving in deed, not just in word)
Revelation 21:1-4 (new heavens and a new earth)

Notes

Chapter 1: Hunger

1. *Time,* November 11, 1974.
2. Moritz Thomsen, *Living Poor* (Seattle: University of Washington Press, 1969), pp. 83–84.

Chapter 2: Food Production

1. Addeke H. Boerma, foreword to *The State of Food and Agriculture 1971,* published by FAO.
2. Patti Hagan, "The Singular Krill," *The New York Times Magazine,* March 9, 1975.
3. Addeke H. Boerma, keynote address to the Second World Food Congress, The Hague, June 16, 1970.

Chapter 3: Population

1. Paul R. and Anne H. Ehrlich, "Misconceptions," *The New York Times Magazine,* June 16, 1974.
2. Barry Commoner, *The Closing Circle* (New York: Knopf, 1972), pp. 243–44.
3. "Pragmatic Immorality," *The New York Times,* January 5, 1975.

Chapter 4: "Haves" and "Have Nots"

1. Peter F. Drucker, *Landmarks of Tomorrow* (New York: Harper & Row, 1959), pp. 160–61.

2. Dennis Bloodworth, *An Eye for the Dragon, Southeast Asia Observed: 1954–1970* (New York: Farrar, Straus & Giroux, 1970), p. 78.
3. Source: U.S. Department of Agriculture, 1984.
4. Georg A. Borgstrom, ''The Dual Challenge of Health and Hunger—A Global Crisis,'' Population Reference Bureau, January 1970.
5. Lester B. Pearson, ''Conflicting Perspectives on the Development Problem: An Introduction,'' *Journal of International Affairs*, No. 2, 1970, p. 159.
6. *Ibid.*, p. 163.

Chapter 5: Environment, Resources and Growth

1. *The New York Times,* June 21, 1970.
2. Paul G. Hoffman, farewell address as Administrator of UN Development Program, October 14, 1971.
3. Barry Commoner, ''Motherhood in Stockholm,'' *Harper's Magazine,* June 1972.

Chapter 6: Up from Hunger

1. Paul E. Johnson, address to the Commission on World Hunger of the Lutheran Church—Missouri Synod, September 24, 1970.
2. Interview with Gerald Leach, ''Can World Technology Stave Off Mass Famine?'' *Chicago Sun-Times,* April 30, 1972.
3. René Dumont and Paul Rosier, *The Hungry Future* (New York: Praeger, 1969), p. 162.
4. Rutherford M. Poats, *Development Cooperation* (Washington: Organization for Economic Cooperation and Development, 1983), p. 13.

Chapter 7: The Rediscovery of America

1. Gunnar Myrdal, *Asian Drama: An Inquiry into the Poverty of Nations* (New York: Pantheon, 1968), volume I, pp. 169–70.

2. Cited by J. William Fulbright, *The Arrogance of Power* (New York: Vintage Books, 1966), p. 115.
3. *The New York Times,* April 24, 1971.
4. J. William Fulbright, *The Arrogance of Power,* as cited, p. 85.
5. A message from U.S. Ambassador Edward Korry to Chilean president Eduardo Frei cited in the U.S. Senate Interim Report of the Select Committee to Study Governmental Operations, *Alleged Assassination Plots Involving Foreign Leaders,* GPO, 1975, page 231.

Chapter 8: Hunger USA

1. Ernest F. Hollings, *The Case Against Hunger* (New York: Cowles, 1970), p. 22.

Chapter 9: Trade: A Hunger Issue

1. Vernon Duckworth-Barker, *Breakthrough to Tomorrow: The Story of International Co-operation for Developmnent through the United Nations* (New York: United Nations, 1970), pp. 48–49.
2. *Partners in Development: Report of the Commission on International Development,* Lester B. Pearson, Chairman (New York: Praeger, 1969), p. 45.
3. David Ross, "New Hope for Latin America?" *The New Republic,* November 22, 1969.
4. Editorial, "Nixon and the New, New, New Look of Aid," *The Christian Century,* September 30, 1970.
5. John K. Jessup, *Life,* March 27, 1970.

Chapter 10: The Role of Investment Abroad

1. Gunnar Myrdal, *The Challenge of World Poverty* (New York: Pantheon, 1970), p. 455.

Chapter 11: Foreign Aid: A Case for Reform

1. *Focus on Poverty* (Washington: World Bank, 1982), p. i.

Chapter 12: Let Them Eat Missiles

1. Robert S. McNamara, in a report to the Board of Governors of the International Bank for Reconstruction and Development, September 21, 1970.
2. Brandt Commission, *Common Crisis: North-South Cooperation for World Recovery* (Cambridge: MIT Press, 1983), p. 43.
3. Interview by Henry Brandon, "Robert McNamara's New Sense of Mission," *The New York Times Magazine,* November 9, 1969.
4. Editorial, "Planning for Peace," *The Progressive,* May 1961.
5. Results reported in "Defense Spending, Economic Structure, and Growth: Evidence Among Countries and Over Time," by Riccardo Faini, Patricia Annez and Lance Taylor, in *Economic Development and Cultural Change* (The University of Chicago Press), April 1984, pp. 487–98.
6. Introduction to the Brandt Commission report, *North–South: A Program for Survival* (Cambridge: MIT Press, 1980), p. 14.
7. Address entitled, "The Chance for Peace," before the American Society of Newspaper Editors on April 16, 1953.

Chapter 13: A Citizens' Movement

1. Mark O. Hatfield, "World Hunger—The Religious Connection," *Worldview,* October 1974.
2. Pope Paul VI, apostolic letter to Cardinal Maurice Roy, May 14, 1971.
3. Gunnar Myrdal, *The Challenge of World Poverty,* as cited, p. 76.

Appendix I

The Right to Food

A statement of policy by Bread for the World, adopted by the board of directors in May 1975 and presented here in abridged form.

Our response to the hunger crisis springs from God's love for all people. By creating us and redeeming us through Jesus Christ, he has given us a love that will not turn aside from those who lack daily bread. The human wholeness of all of us—the well-fed as well as the starving—is at stake.

As Christians we affirm the right to food: the right of every man, woman, and child on earth to a nutritionally adequate diet. This right is grounded in the value God places on human life and in the belief that "the earth is the Lord's and the fulness thereof." Because other considerations, including the importance of work, flow from these, we cannot rest until the fruit of God's earth is shared in a way that befits his human family.

Today hundreds of millions suffer from acute hunger. For this reason Bread for the World supports the work of church and other agencies in alleviating hunger, and urges increased support for them. However, the problem is far too massive for private agencies alone. The resources that governments command must also be used if food is to reach people in most areas of famine and end starvation.

But emergency aid is not enough. We need to think in terms of *long-range strategies* that deal with the causes of hunger. These causes include poverty, illiteracy, lack of health services, technical inadequacy, rapid growth of population, and unemployment, to name some of the more serious. Church relief agencies have increasingly sponsored development projects that address these problems. But again, although there are small models of excellence on the part of those agencies, the extent of hunger makes large-scale government assistance essential.

Hunger is also rooted in privileges that may, in securing wealth for some, perpetuate the poverty of others. Because they reflect sinful human nature and are usually sanctioned by custom and law, these privileges are often the most obstinate causes of hunger. The rich can resist taxes that could generate jobs for the poor. Landless peasants may be forced to work for a few pennies an hour. Tenant farmers are often kept in perpetual debt. The powerful, with privileges to protect, can use repression to prevent change.

The problem of privileges for some at the cost of hunger for others applies not only to persons and groups within a country, but also to nations. Because the United States earns more than twice the income of the entire poor world, U.S. Christians need to be especially alert to the possibility that our privileges may come at high cost to others.

The policies of the U.S. government are especially crucial regarding world hunger. Our nation can lead countless persons out of hunger or lock them into despair and death. Citizen impact on U.S. policies is, therefore, our most important tool in the struggle against hunger.

In affirming the right to food, Bread for the World seeks:

1. *An end to hunger in the United States.* It supports:

A. a floor of economic decency under every U.S. citizen through measures such as a minimum income and guaranteed employment;

B. steps to improve existing programs, such as (1) food stamps; (2) school lunches; and (3) nutritional assistance for especially vulnerable persons, along with steps to enroll in these programs all who qualify; and

C. a national nutrition policy that enables every citizen to get an acceptably nutritious diet.

2. *A U.S. food policy committed to world food security and rural development, as proposed by the World Food Conference.*

The United States clearly shoulders a special responsibility regarding global food needs. Our country controls most of the world's grain exports.

The World Food Conference charted the necessary path to world food security under a World Food Council that would coordinate both emergency relief efforts and long-range rural development. Bread for the World supports:

A. U.S. participation in a world food reserve program, with reserves under national control;

B. an increase in U.S. food assistance, especially the grant portion, as our share toward the establishment of a grain reserve with an initial world target of 10 million tons;

C. humanitarian, not political, use of food assistance;

D. a fair return to the U.S. farmer for his production, with curbs against windfall profits and special measures to assist family farmers; just wages for farm workers; and

E. full U.S. participation in the International Fund for Agricultural Development, along with other steps that would promote rural development in the poor countries. Such development would, among other things, enable them to produce or secure adequate supplies of fertilizer and energy, and accelerate research relating to food production there.

3. *The reform and expansion of U.S. development assistance.*

The United States currently ranks near the bottom of Development Assistance Committee nations, when assistance is measured as a percentage of GNP. By official (and somewhat exaggerated) figures, U.S. development assistance to poor countries amounts to one-fifth of 1 percent of our GNP. We can do better than that. What is true for the United States is true for all countries: "To whom much has been given, much will be required." Further, the *quality* of assistance is crucial. Assistance should deliver self-help opportunities primarily to those living in hunger and poverty, especially the rural poor. It should be aimed at developing self-reliance, not dependency on the part of the recipient nations and people. And rather than imposing capital-intensive western technologies on those countries, assistance should make possible the development of locally appropriate technologies, usually geared to small-scale, labor-intensive methods. Bread for the World therefore supports:

A. a U.S. contribution, in proportion to our share of the world's income, to the International Fund for Agricultural Development as a major attempt to increase the food production capacity and living standards of impoverished rural families;

B. rapid movement toward the 1-percent-of-GNP assistance goal;

C. the "untying" of assistance. Economic strings that put burdens on recipient nations should be cut;

D. channeling of development assistance through international and transnational agencies, where possible, without precluding the expansion of bilateral assistance; and

E. adoption, with other donor and recipient nations, of an internationally agreed set of standards on the basis of which the amount of development assistance would be determined. These standards should include: (a) need; (b) evidence that development is occurring among the masses of poor people; (c) willingness of leaders to institute basic reforms, such as land reform, tax reform, and anti-corruption measures, in order to reduce the disparity between rich and poor within a country; (d) de-emphasis on military spending; and (e) efforts to secure human rights.

4. *The separation of development assistance from all forms of military assistance.*

Most U.S. aid is either military assistance or assistance in which political and military considerations are uppermost. This mixing of humanitarian assistance with military and political aid gives the public an exaggerated impression of real U.S. aid to hungry and poverty-ridden countries. Bread for the World therefore proposes legislation to sever completely the connection between humanitarian development assistance and military and political assistance.

5. *Trade preferences for the poorest countries.*

Trade is not perceived by the public as a "hunger" issue, but trade, even more than aid, vitally affects hungry people. In the past poor countries have been compelled to export their raw materials at bargain prices, and import high-priced manufactured products. The terms of such trade have progressively deteriorated over the past two decades. Recent food, fertilizer, and oil price hikes have left the 40 poorest countries, representing a billion people, in a desperate position. For them in particular trade opportunities are more important than ever. Bread for the World therefore supports the following positions, which are partly embodied in the Trade Act of 1974:

A. the lowering of trade barriers such as tariffs and quotas, especially on semi-processed and finished products. It has been estimated that these barriers cost U.S. consumers $10 to $15 billion a year;

B. special trade preferences for the poorest countries. These countries need markets for their products, if they are to work their way out of hunger; and

C. greatly increased planning for economic adjustment, including assistance for adversely affected U.S. workers and industries. Without this, U.S. laborers are made to bear an unfair burden and are increasingly pitted against hungry people.

6. *Reduced military spending.*

U.S. defense spending alone exceeds the total annual income of the poorest billion people on earth, the truly hungry children of God. Our thinking begins with them. During his presidential years, Dwight D. Eisenhower said, "Every gun that is made, every warship launched, every rocket fired signifies, in the final sense, a theft from those who hunger and are not fed, those who are cold and are not clothed." Bread for the World supports:

A. greater U.S. initiative in pressing for arms limitation agreements and mutual cutbacks in existing arms as well as greater public access to information surrounding negotiations;

B. curtailment of the sale of arms, if possible by international agreement; and

C. adoption of a U.S. defense budget that would reduce military spending. For example, a 10 percent reduction could provide $9 billion* for financing long-range measures against hunger.

7. *Study and appropriate control of multinational corporations, with particular attention to agribusiness.*

Multinationals are playing an increasingly influential global role. They transcend national boundaries and often bring jobs and needed development opportunities to poor countries. But they create empires that are not accountable to host countries and often impose a type of development that reinforces inequalities and, consequently, the problem of hunger, as well. Bread for the World therefore supports:

A. the principle that each country has the right to determine its own path to human and social development, including legitimate control over outside investments;

*By 1984 it was $24 billion.

B. efforts to study and analyze the role of multinational corporations, especially as they relate positively or negatively to the problem of hunger;

C. national and international measures that seek fair means of accountability on the part of such companies; and

D. special examination of the role of corporate farming, with a view toward adequate safeguards for low-income consumers and small family farm holders.

8. *Efforts to deal with the population growth rate.*

Rapid population growth is putting great pressure on the world's food supply and on the capacity of countries to absorb the increase into their economies. Population growth will not be effectively curbed if it is dealt with in isolation, but only if placed in the context of total development needs. For example, hungry people usually have large families, in part because surviving sons provide security in old age. Only where social and economic gains include the poor, and where the rate of infant mortality begins to approximate that of the affluent nations, do people feel secure enough to limit family size. Bread for the World therefore supports:

A. greatly expanded U.S. efforts to enable the poor of the world to work their way out of hunger and poverty;

B. additional U.S. assistance for health programs abroad aimed at reducing infant mortality and increasing health security;

C. additional support for research to develop family planning methods that are dependable, inexpensive, simple, safe, and morally acceptable to all; and

D. efforts to modify our own consumption, which strains the carrying capacity of the earth no less than population increases.

9. *Christian patterns of living.*

The growing scarcity of several key resources—grain, fuel, and fertilizer in particular—that directly affect the food supply has prompted many to reassess their habits of consumption. This country, with 6 percent of the world's population, consumes one-third or more of the world's marketed resources. On the average each person in the United States buys about 4.5 times more grain—most of it indirectly as meat and dairy products, along with alcohol and pet food—than persons in poor countries do. There is often no direct connection between our using less and others having more. Nevertheless there are important psychological, symbolic, and spiritual values in reexamining our patterns of consumption. Bread for the World invites Christians to:

A. remember that along with changes in habits of consumption we have to change government policies, without which life-style modifications do little more than give us a misleading sense of accomplishment;

B. reconsider our personal spending and consuming, with a view toward living more simply and less materialistically;

C. reconsider a way of life in which billions of dollars are spent annually to make us crave, and in turn spend countless additional billions on products we do not need, and which in fact often harm us—all this while sisters and brothers perish for lack of bread.

These things we seek because we affirm for others a right that we enjoy: the right to food. We seek to extend to all this God-given right in obedience to Christ who has called us to follow him in loving our neighbor as ourselves.

Appendix II

The Right to Food Resolution

As passed by the U.S. Senate (S. Con. Res. 138) on September 16, 1976. The U.S. House of Representatives passed a similar resolution on September 21, 1976.

WHEREAS in this Bicentennial Year we reaffirm our national commitment to the inalienable right of all to life, liberty, and the pursuit of happiness, none of which can be realized without food to adequately sustain and nourish life, and we recall that the right to food and freedom from hunger was set forth in the Universal Declaration of Human Rights and in the World Food Conference Declaration of 1974, and

WHEREAS the report entitled "The Assessment of the World Food Situation," prepared for the 1974 World Food Conference, estimated that four hundred and sixty million persons, almost half of them young children, are malnourished; and

WHEREAS nearly half of the human race lives on diets seriously deficient in proteins or other essential nutrients; and

WHEREAS most of this hunger and malnutrition is suffered by the poor in developing countries whose poverty prevents them from obtaining adequate food; and

WHEREAS the demand for food is accelerating and the unprecedented growth in population will add a billion persons to the world's population in less than 15 years; and

WHEREAS the Food and Agriculture Organization, and other recognized authorities, currently estimate that by 1985 the developing countries will experience an annual food deficit of 85 million tons; and

WHEREAS it is in the interest of the United States and all nations to overcome food shortages which cause human suffering and generate economic and political instability; and

WHEREAS the United States proposed, and all nations at the World Food Conference of 1974 accepted, the bold objective "that within a decade no child will go to bed hungry, that no family will fear for its next day's bread, and that no human being's future and capacities will be stunted by malnutrition"; and

WHEREAS the international community has repeatedly urged the industrialized nations to increase their official development assistance to 0.7 percent of their total national production (GNP); and

WHEREAS the elimination of global hunger and malnutrition cannot succeed without expanded self-help efforts by the developing countries: Now, therefore, be it

RESOLVED by the House of Representatives (the Senate concurring), That it is the sense of Congress that

(1) the United States reaffirms the right of every person in this country and throughout the world to food and a nutritionally adequate diet; and

(2) the need to combat hunger shall be a fundamental point of reference in the formulation and implementation of United States policy in all areas which bear on hunger including international trade, monetary arrangements, and foreign assistance; and

(3) in the United States, we should seek to improve food assistance programs for all those who are in need, to ensure that all eligible recipients have the opportunity to receive a nutritionally adequate diet, and to reduce unemployment and ensure a level of economic decency for everyone; and

(4) the United States should emphasize and expand its assistance for self-help development among the world's poorest people, especially in countries seriously affected by hunger and malnutrition, with particular emphasis on increasing food production and encouraging more equitable patterns of food distribution and economic growth; and such assistance, in order to be effective, should be coordinated with expanded efforts by international organizations, donor nations, and the recipient countries to provide a nutritionally adequate diet for all.

Appendix III

Questions for Group Discussion

The biblical references at the end of chapter 14 may be useful in connection with group discussion.

Chapter 1: Hunger

1. How important is it to sense emotionally the suffering of hungry people? What are some of the pluses and minuses involved?

2. Why have Christians been so relief-oriented, but so reluctant to influence public policy on the hunger issue?

3. Joseph's role in Egypt as the "Secretary of Agriculture" offers an interesting precedent (Genesis 39ff). What can we learn from this piece of biblical history?

4. What responses does the World Food Conference suggest to us as individuals and as a nation?

Chapter 2: Food Production

1. What bearing does the biblical teaching of stewardship have on the question of food production and distribution? (See, for example, Genesis 1:27 and Matthew 25:14–30.)

2. On Sundays many Christians echo the vision of the prophet Isaiah when they sing; "Heaven and earth are filled with your glory." Can we say this to a person in Tanzania or the Sahel who is slowly wasting away from hunger?

3. In the same setting, how are we to understand the words of Jesus (Matthew 6), "Do not be anxious, saying, 'What shall we eat?' or

'What shall we drink?' . . . But seek first his kingdom and his justice, and all these things shall be yours as well''?

4. Discuss some of the topics treated in this chapter.

Chapter 3: Population

1. Has reading this chapter changed your views in any way?

2. If hunger and poverty play a key role in spurring population growth, why is it that so many U.S. citizens think of birth control programs as the lone answer?

3. What light does the experience of poor countries shed on this problem?

4. What do *you* think about the ''lifeboat'' and ''triage'' theories?

5. What biblical teachings address these matters?

Chapter 4: "Haves" and "Have Nots"

1. What is the special situation of today's poor countries?

2. Why is it important for us to understand this?

3. What place does charity have in our response?

4. What place does justice have in our response?

Chapter 5: Environment, Resources and Growth

1. This chapter illustrates the danger of grabbing quick, oversimplified answers. What do we do when the evidence is mixed, and good causes conflict?

2. How do the poor and hungry fit into our thinking in cases like that?

3. Discuss the relationship between life style and public policy.

4. What biblical resources can we draw on for our understanding of issues posed in this chapter?

Chapter 6: Up from Hunger

1. What impact, good or bad, has the desire of people in poor countries to imitate the West had on development in those countries?

2. What type of development do you think is most human, most in keeping with the justice that reflects God's rule?

3. Would you apply to yourself and to our country the type of development you think is best for others?

4. Can we speak of a "Christian" economic system?

5. Why has agriculture been so neglected in poor countries? If we are urban dwellers, do we have any bias against agriculture that might help to explain this problem?

Chapter 7: The Rediscovery of America

1. What is the relationship between the U.S. ideals of liberty and justice, and biblical themes of liberty and justice? What are the dangers of confusing the two? Of breaking all connections between the two?

2. How do U.S. ideals relate to the problem of hunger?

3. What biblical examples or insights help us understand how a nation should use its power?

4. As Christians we hold a dual citizenship—in heaven, Paul stressed (Phil. 3:20); but he also used his Roman citizenship effectively (Acts 22:22–29; 25:11–12). What does such dual citizenship mean to us, as we respond to world hunger?

Chapter 8: Hunger USA

1. Why *are* people hungry in the United States?

2. To what extent is the physical separation of most of us from hungry people in our own area a matter of accident, and to what extent is it by deliberate choice?

3. What could you do with others to assist hungry people in your area?

4. Discuss the self-contempt and self-righteousness that so easily afflict the poor and the nonpoor. What does the Gospel have to say about the way we see ourselves and the way we see others?

5. What do we have to offer the hungry? What do they have to offer us?

Chapter 9: Trade: A Hunger Issue

1. Discuss the oil crisis as it might look (a) to people from a Middle Eastern oil-exporting country; (b) to people from a non-oil-producing poor country.

2. To what extent do trade arrangements tend to perpetuate inequalities and therefore hunger?

3. How might trade preferences affect people in the United States?

4. What does this have to do with Christian faith?

Chapter 10: The Role of Investment Abroad

1. Is profit-making inescapably at odds with development needs? Or naturally in harmony? What are the implications of our answer(s)?

2. Nationalism is a powerful force. How does it come into play in the matter of international business from the U.S. side of the picture? From the side of the poor countries?

3. What realistic steps could be taken to deal with the rising indebtedness of poor countries?

4. How does the biblical teaching of stewardship relate to the question of investment?

Chapter 11: Foreign Aid: A Case for Reform

1. What has changed since the years of massive assistance following World War II—U.S. generosity or the situation?

2. Discuss the difficulties of being a donor nation; of being a recipient nation.

3. What should assistance seek to accomplish and what should it avoid?

4. Discuss the question of charity and justice in relation to foreign aid.

Chapter 12: Let Them Eat Missiles

1. Can Christians be realists when dealing with the question of military needs? If so, or if not, what does that mean?

2. Discuss the danger of seeing things from the perspective of a specialist—say, that of a Defense Department official; or of an industrialist; or of a worker in a defense industry. Even if we are none of these, how might our own point of view be heavily slanted one way or another?

3. One danger is that we "leave this up to the experts," another that we jump to oversimplified conclusions. How do we avoid these dangers?

Chapter 13: A Citizens' Movement

1. How do you explain the reluctance of Christians to offer their citizenship in helping hungry people?

2. Jesus said, "My kingdom is not of this world." Does that mean this world is not part of his kingdom?

3. Discuss the possibilities of forming a public-policy-oriented group in your congregation, neighborhood or area.

Chapter 14: "What Can I Do?"

1. Discuss what you can do as individuals and as a group.

Appendix IV

217

Alice Gallin, O.S.U.
Executive Director, Association
of Catholic Colleges and
Universities

Allyson George
BFW Metro-Coordinator,
Pittsburgh

J. Bryan Hehir
Director, Office of International
Justice and Peace, U.S. Catholic
Conference

John F. Hohenstein
Coordinator, BFW Metro
Council, Philadelphia

Tom Hunsdorfer
Associate Director, Chrysalis
Program, Christian Theological
Seminary

JoAnne H. Kagiwada
Director, International Affairs,
Christian Church (Disciples of
Christ)

Mwangi Karangu
Chairperson, Department of
Economics, Morgan State
University

Norma J. Kehrberg
Associate General Secretary,
United Methodist Committee on
Relief (UMCOR)

Othal H. Lakey
Presiding Bishop, 2nd Episcopal
District, C.M.E. Church,
Cincinnati, Ohio

William A. Lawson
Pastor, Wheeler Avenue
Baptist Church,
Houston, Texas

Andy Loving
Director of Street Ministries,
St. Luke's Episcopal Church,
Atlanta

Charles Lutz
Director, Office of Church in
Society, American Lutheran
Church

David L. McKenna
President, Asbury Theological
Seminary

Gwendolyn Massey
Coordinator, Refugee and Relief
Services, Church of God,
Anderson, Indiana

Stan Mooneyham
Feed the Children

P. Francis Murphy
Auxiliary Bishop of Baltimore

Victoria P. Oshiro
BFW State Coordinator,
Minnesota

I WANT TO BECOME A

☐ **Member at $25 a year (if this fee is a financial hardship for you, please contribute what you can)**

☐ **Contributor (individual or church) at:**
    ☐ **$100 a year**
    ☐ **$10 a month**
    ☐ **other $_____**

☐ **Send more information**

NAME_____

ADDRESS_____

CITY_____**STATE**_____**ZIP**_____

PHONE (home)_____**(work)**_____

RELIGIOUS AFFILIATION_____

OCCUPATION_____

REPRESENTATIVE_____

BREAD FOR THE WORLD
802 Rhode Island Avenue, N.E.
Washington, D.C. 20018